Best True Cat Stories

Best True Cat Stories

Edited by

Karen Dolan

Michael O'Mara Books Limited

First published in 2001 by
Michael O'Mara Books Limited
9 Lion Yard
Tremadoc Road
London SW4 7NQ

Copyright © 2001 by Michael O'Mara Books Limited

A CIP catalogue record for this book is available from the
British Library.

ISBN 1-85479-865-0

1 3 5 7 9 10 8 6 4 2

Designed and typeset by DW Design

Printed and bound by Cox & Wyman, Reading

Contents

MRS BOND'S CATS by James Herriot   1

MEMOIR OF THE CATS OF GRETA HALL
    by Robert Southey   10

INCIDENT ON EAST NINTH by Jill Drower   19

JEREMY BENTHAM'S CAT by John Bowring   28

THE CONSCIENTIOUS CAT by Agnes A. Sandham   30

THE BLACK CAT OF KILLAKEE by Daniel Cohen   36

CATS OF MY CHILDHOOD by May Eustace   39

JUNO by Harriet Beecher Stowe   50

THE CHERRY TREE by Derek Tangye   53

CALVIN, THE CAT by Charles Dudley Warner   66

CATS THAT SWAM AND CYCLED
    by N. Teulon Porter   78

THE LEGAL VALUE OF A CAT   82

MOPPET by Dominique Enright   84

ALAS, POOR TIDDLES, WE KNEW HIM WELL...
    by Andrew Parsons   86

STRANGE FRIENDS by Mark Twain   91

NELSON, THE BRAVE   92

MY BOSS THE CAT by Paul Gallico   93

THE CAT BY THE FIRE by Leigh Hunt   98

WAITING FOR THE BAR TO OPEN
    by Carl Van Vechten   106

THE FAT CAT by Q. Patrick   108

JUBILATE AGNO by Christopher Smart   114

RUFUS THE SURVIVOR by Doris Lessing   118

WHITE HOUSE CAT by Theodore Roosevelt   139

WILD WALES by George Borrow   141

CAT BURGLARS by Jacquie Wines   145

THE ACHIEVEMENT OF THE CAT by Saki   148

MINNA MINNA MOWBRAY by Michael Joseph   150

THE WORSHIPFUL CAT   169

THE CAT WITH THE WOODEN PAW
     by Wendell Margrave   172

STORMY, THE LONG-DISTANCE CAT   173

THE UNDOING OF MORNING GLORY ADOLPHUS

by N. Margaret Campbell   174

U.S. MILITARY 0, CATS 1   180

A VET'S LIFE by John Bower   181

THE HOME LIFE OF A HOLY CAT
     by Arthur Wiegall   190

THE WHITE AND BLACK DYNASTIES
     by Théophile Gautier   199

MIN AND THE MOUSE by Henry David Thoreau   210

DISCIPLINE by Agnes Repplier   211

MIDSHIPMAN, THE CAT by John Coleman Adams   212

FELINE AFFECTION Anon   223

SOLOMON AND SHEBA by Doreen Tovey   225

CATS OF HONOUR
     by General Sir Thomas Edward Gordon   242

DR JOHNSON'S CAT   244

ACKNOWLEDGMENTS   246

Mrs Bond's Cats

JAMES HERRIOT

'I work for cats.' That was how Mrs Bond introduced herself on my first visit, gripping my hand firmly and thrusting out her jaw defiantly as though challenging me to make something of it. She was a big woman with a strong, high-cheekboned face and a commanding presence and I wouldn't have argued with her anyway, so I nodded gravely as though I fully understood and agreed, and allowed her to lead me into the house.

I saw at once what she meant. The big kitchen-living room had been completely given over to cats. There were cats on the sofas and chairs and spilling in cascades on to the floor, cats sitting in rows along the window sills and, right in the middle of it all, little Mr Bond, pallid, wispy-moustached, in his shirt sleeves reading a newspaper.

It was a scene which was going to become very familiar. A lot of the cats were obviously uncastrated Toms because the atmosphere was vibrant with their distinctive smell – a fierce pungency which overwhelmed even the sickly wisps from the big saucepans of nameless cat food bubbling on the stove. And Mr Bond was always there, always in his shirt sleeves and reading his paper, a lonely little island in a sea of cats.

I had heard of the Bonds, of course. They were Londoners who for some obscure reason had picked on North Yorkshire for their retirement. People said they had a 'bit o' brass' and they had bought an old house on the outskirts of Darrowby where they kept themselves to themselves – and the cats. I had heard that Mrs Bond was in the habit of taking in strays and feeding them and giving them a home if they wanted it and this had predisposed me in her favour, because in my experience the unfortunate feline species seemed to be fair game for every kind of cruelty and neglect. They shot cats, threw things at them, starved them and set their dogs on them for fun. It was good to see somebody taking their side.

My patient on this first visit was no more than a big kitten, terrified little blob of black and white crouching in a corner.

'He's one of the outside cats,' Mrs Bond boomed.

'Outside cats?'

'Yes. All these you see here are the inside cats. The others are the really wild ones who simply refuse to enter the house. I feed them of course but the only time they come indoors is when they are ill.'

'I see.'

'I've had frightful trouble catching this one. I'm worried about his eyes – there seemed to be a skin growing over them, and I do hope you can do something for him. His name, by the way, is Alfred.'

'Alfred? Ah yes, quite.' I advanced cautiously on the little half-grown animal and was greeted by a waving set of claws and a series of open-mouthed spittings. He was trapped in his corner or he would have been off with the speed of light.

Examining him was going to be a problem. I turned to Mrs Bond. 'Could you let me have a sheet of some kind? An old ironing sheet would do. I'm going to have to wrap him up.'

'Wrap him up?' Mrs Bond looked very doubtful but

she disappeared into another room and returned with a tattered sheet of cotton which looked just right.

I cleared the table of an amazing variety of cat feeding dishes, cat books, cat medicines and spread out the sheet, then I approached my patient again. You can't be in a hurry in a situation like this and it took me perhaps five minutes of wheedling and 'Puss-pussing' while I brought my hand nearer and nearer. When I got as far as being able to stroke his cheek I made a quick grab at the scruff of his neck and finally bore Alfred, protesting bitterly and lashing out in all directions, over to the table. There, still holding tightly to his scruff, I laid him on the sheet and started the wrapping operation.

This is something which has to be done quite often with obstreperous felines and, although I say it, I am rather good at it. The idea is to make a neat, tight roll, leaving the relevant piece of cat exposed; it may be an injured paw, perhaps the tail, and in this case of course the head. I think it was the beginning of Mrs Bond's unquestioning faith in me when she saw me quickly enveloping that cat till all you could see of him was a small black and white head protruding from an immovable cocoon of cloth. He and I were now facing each other, more or less eyeball to eyeball, and Alfred couldn't do a thing about it.

As I say, I rather pride myself on this little expertise and even today my veterinary colleagues have been known to remark: 'Old Herriot may be limited in many respects but by God he can wrap a cat.'

As it turned out, there wasn't a skin growing over Alfred's eyes. There never is.

'He's got a paralysis of the third eyelid, Mrs Bond. Animals have this membrane which flicks across the eye to protect it. In this case it hasn't gone back, probably because the cat is in low condition – maybe had a touch of cat flu or something else which has weakened him. I'll give him an injection of vitamins and leave you some powder to put in his food if you could keep him in for a few days. I think he'll be all right in a week or two.'

The injection presented no problems with Alfred furious but helpless inside his sheet and I had come to the end of my first visit to Mrs Bond's.

It was the first of many. The lady and I established an immediate rapport which was strengthened by the fact that I was always prepared to spend time over her assorted charges; crawling on my stomach under piles of logs in the outhouses to reach the outside cats, coaxing them down from trees, stalking them endlessly through the shrubbery. But from my point of view it was rewarding in many ways.

For instance there was the diversity of names she had for her cats. True to her London upbringing she had named many of the Toms after the great Arsenal team of those days. There was Eddie Hapgood, Cliff Bastin, Ted Drake, Wilf Copping, but she did slip up in one case because Alex James had kittens three times a year with unfailing regularity.

Then there was her way of calling them home. The first time I saw her at this was on a still summer evening. The two cats she wanted me to see were out in the garden somewhere and I walked with her to the back door where she halted, clasped her hands across her bosom, closed her eyes and gave tongue in a mellifluous contralto.

'Bates, Bates, Bates, Ba-hates.' She actually sang out the words in a reverent monotone except for a delightful little lilt on the 'Ba-hates'. Then once more she inflated her ample rib cage like an operatic prima donna and out it came again, delivered with the utmost feeling.

'Bates, Bates, Bates, Ba-hates.'

Anyway it worked, because Bates the cat came trotting from behind a clump of laurel. There remained the other patient and I watched Mrs Bond with interest.

She took up the same stance, breathed in, closed her

eyes, composed her features into a sweet half-smile and started again.

'Seven-times-three, Seven-times-three, Seven-times-threehee.' It was set to the same melody as Bates with the same dulcet rise and fall at the end. She didn't get the quick response this time, though, and had to go through the performance again and again, and as the notes lingered on the still evening air the effect was startlingly like a muezzin calling the faithful to prayer.

At length she was successful and a fat tortoiseshell slunk apologetically along the wall-side into the house.

'By the way, Mrs Bond,' I asked, making my voice casual. 'I didn't quite catch the name of that last cat.'

'Oh, Seven-times-three?' She smiled reminiscently. 'Yes, she is a dear. She's had three kittens seven times running, you see, so I thought it rather a good name for her, don't you?'

'Yes, yes, I do indeed. Splendid name, splendid.'

Another thing which warmed me towards Mrs Bond was her concern for my safety. I appreciated this because it is a rare trait among animal owners. I can think of the trainer after one of his racehorses had kicked me clean out of a loose box examining the animal anxiously to see if it had damaged its foot; the little old lady dwarfed by the bristling, teeth-bared Alsatian saying: 'You'll be gentle with him won't you and I hope you won't hurt him – he's very nervous'; the farmer, after an exhausting calving which I feel certain has knocked about two years off my life expectancy, grunting morosely: 'I doubt you've tired that cow out, young man.'

Mrs Bond was different. She used to meet me at the door with an enormous pair of gauntlets to protect my hands against scratches and it was an inexpressible relief to find that somebody cared. It became part of the pattern of my life; walking up the garden path among the innumerable slinking, wild-eyed little creatures which were the outside cats, the ceremonial acceptance of the gloves at the door, then the entry into the charged atmosphere of the kitchen with little Mr Bond and his newspaper just visible among the milling furry bodies of the inside cats. I was never able to ascertain Mr Bond's attitude to cats – come to think of it he hardly ever said anything – but I had the impression he could take them or leave them.

The gauntlets were a big help and at times they were a veritable godsend. As in the case of Boris. Boris was an enormous blue-black member of the outside cats and my bête noire in more senses than one. I always cherished a private conviction that he had escaped from a zoo; I had never seen a domestic cat with such sleek, writhing muscles, such dedicated ferocity. I'm sure there was a bit of puma in Boris somewhere.

It had been a sad day for the cat colony when he turned up. I have always found it difficult to dislike any animal; most of the ones which try to do us a mischief are activated by fear, but Boris was different; he was a malevolent bully and after his arrival the frequency of my visits increased because of his habit of regularly beating up his colleagues. I was forever stitching up tattered ears, dressing gnawed limbs.

We had one trial of strength fairly early. Mrs Bond wanted me to give him a worm dose and I had the little tablet all ready held in forceps. How I ever got hold of him I don't quite know, but I hustled him on to the table and did my wrapping act at lightning speed, swathing him in roll upon roll of stout material. Just for a few seconds I thought I had him as he stared up at me, his great brilliant eyes full of hate. But as I pushed my loaded forceps into his mouth he clamped his teeth viciously down on them and I could feel claws of amazing power tearing inside the sheet. It was all over in moments. A long leg shot out and ripped its way down my wrist, I let go my tight hold of the neck and in a flash Boris sank his teeth through the gauntlet into the ball of my thumb and was away. I was left standing there stupidly, holding the fragmented worm tablet in a bleeding hand and looking at the bunch of ribbons which had once been my wrapping sheet. From then on Boris loathed the very sight of me and the feeling was mutual.

But this was one of the few clouds in a serene sky. I continued to enjoy my visits there and life proceeded on a tranquil course except, perhaps, for some legpulling from my colleagues. They could never understand my willingness to spend so much time over a lot of cats. And of course this fitted in with the general attitude because Siegfried didn't believe in people keeping pets of any kind. He just couldn't understand their mentality and propounded his views to anybody who cared to listen. He himself, of course, kept five dogs and two cats. The dogs, all of them, travelled everywhere with him in the car and he fed dogs and cats every day with his own hands – wouldn't allow anybody else to do the job. In the evening all seven animals would pile themselves round his feet as he sat in his chair by the fire. To this day he is still as vehemently anti-pet as ever, though another generation of waving dogs' tails almost obscures him as he drives around and he also has several cats, a few tanks of tropical fish and a couple of snakes.

Tristan saw me in action at Mrs Bond's on only one occasion. I was collecting some long forceps from the instrument cupboard when he came into the room.

'Anything interesting, Jim?' he asked.

'No, not really. I'm just off to see one of the Bond cats. It's got a bone stuck between its teeth.'

The young man eyed me ruminatively for a moment. 'Think I'll come with you. I haven't seen much small animal stuff lately.'

As we went down the garden at the cat establishment I felt a twinge of embarrassment. One of the things which had built up my happy relationship with Mrs Bond was

7

my tender concern for her charges. Even with the wildest and the fiercest I exhibited only gentleness, patience and solicitude; it wasn't really an act, it came quite naturally to me. However, I couldn't help wondering what Tristan would think of my cat bedside manner.

Mrs Bond in the doorway had summed up the situation in a flash and had two pairs of gauntlets waiting. Tristan looked a little surprised as he received his pair but thanked the lady with typical charm. He looked still more surprised when he entered the kitchen, sniffed the rich atmosphere and surveyed the masses of furry creatures occupying almost every available inch of space.

'Mr Herriot, I'm afraid it's Boris who has the bone in his teeth,' Mrs Bond said.

'Boris!' My stomach lurched. 'How on earth are we going to catch him?'

'Oh I've been rather clever,' she replied. 'I've managed to entice him with some of his favourite food into a cat basket.'

Tristan put his hand on a big wicker cage on the table. 'In here, is he?' he asked casually. He slipped back the catch and opened the lid. For something like a third of a second the coiled creature within and Tristan regarded each other tensely, then a sleek black body exploded silently from the basket past the young man's left ear on to the top of a tall cupboard.

'Christ!' said Tristan. 'What the hell was that?'

'That,' I said, 'was Boris, and now we've got to get hold of him again.' I climbed on to a chair, reached slowly on to the cupboard top and started 'Puss-puss-puss'ing in my most beguiling tone.

After about a minute Tristan appeared to think he had a better idea; he made a sudden leap and grabbed Boris's tail. But only briefly, because the big cat freed himself in an instant and set off on a whirlwind circuit of the room; along the tops of cupboards and dressers, across the curtains, careering round and round like a wall-of-death rider.

Tristan stationed himself at a strategic point and as Boris shot past he swiped at him with one of the gauntlets.

'Missed the bloody thing!' he shouted in chagrin. 'But here he comes again ... take that, you black sod! Damn it, I can't nail him!'

The docile little inside cats, startled by the scattering of plates and tins and pans and by Tristan's cries and arm wavings, began to run around in their turn, knocking over whatever Boris had missed. The noise and confusion even got through to Mr Bond because just for a moment he raised his head and looked around him in mild surprise at the hurtling bodies before returning to his newspaper.

Tristan, flushed with the excitement of the chase, had really begun to enjoy himself. I cringed inwardly as he shouted over to me happily.

'Send him on, Jim, I'll get the bugger next time round!'

We never did catch Boris. We just had to leave the piece of bone to work its own way out, so it wasn't a successful veterinary visit. But Tristan as we got back into the car smiled contentedly.

'That was great, Jim. I didn't realize you had such fun with your pussies.'

Mrs Bond on the other hand, when I next saw her, was rather tight-lipped over the whole thing.

'Mr Herriot,' she said, 'I hope you aren't going to bring that young man with you again.'

Memoir of the Cats
of Greta Hall

ROBERT SOUTHEY

For as much, most excellent Edith May, as you must always feel a natural and becoming concern in whatever relates to the house wherein you were born, and in which the first part of your life has thus far so happily been spent, I have for your instruction and delight composed these Memoirs of the Cats of Greta Hall: to the end that the memory of such worthy animals may not perish, but be held in deserved honour by my children, and those who shall come after them. And let me not be supposed unmindful of Beelzebub of Bath, and Senhor Thomaz de Lisboa, that I have not gone back to an earlier period, and included them in my design. Far be it from me to intend any injury or disrespect to their shades! Opportunity of doing justice to their virtues will not be wanting at some future time, but for the present I must confine myself within the limits of these precincts.

In the autumn of the year 1803, when I entered upon this place of abode, I found the hearth in possession of two cats, whom my nephew Hartley Coleridge (then in the 7th year of his age) had named Lord Nelson, and Bona Marietta. The former, as the name implies, was of

10

the worthier gender: it is as decidedly so in Cats, as in Grammar and in law. He was an ugly specimen of the streaked-carrotty, or Judas-coloured kind; which is one of the ugliest varieties. But *nimium ne crede colori*. In spite of his complexion, there was nothing treacherous about him. He was altogether a good Cat, affectionate, vigilant and brave; and for services performed against the Rats was deservedly raised in succession to the rank of Baron, Viscount and Earl. He lived to a good old age; and then, being quite helpless and miserable, was in mercy thrown into the river. I had more than once interfered to save him from this fate; but it became at length plainly an act of compassion to consent to it. And here let me observe that in a world wherein death is necessary, the law of nature by which one creature preys upon another is a law of mercy, not only because death is thus made instrumental to life, and more life exists in consequence, but also because it is better for the creatures themselves to be cut off suddenly, than to perish by disease or hunger – for these are the only alternatives.

There are still some of Lord Nelson's descendants in the town of Keswick. Two of the family were handsomer than I should have supposed any Cats of this complexion could have been; but their fur was fine, the colour a rich carrot, and the striping like that of the finest tyger or tabby kind. I named one of them William Rufus; the other Danayr le Roux, after a personage in the Romance of Gyron le Courtoys.

Bona Marietta was the mother of Bona Fidelia, so named by my nephew aforesaid. Bona Fidelia was a tortoiseshell cat. She was filiated upon Lord Nelson, others of the same litter having borne the unequivocal stamp of his likeness. It was in her good qualities that she resembled him, for in truth her name rightly bespoke her nature. She approached as nearly as possible in disposition, to the ideal of a perfect cat: he who supposes that animals have not their difference of disposition as well as men, knows very little of animal nature. Having survived her daughter Madame Catalani, she died of extreme old age, universally esteemed and regretted by all who had the pleasure of her acquaintance.

Bona Fidelia left a daughter and a granddaughter; the former I called Madame Bianchi – the latter Pulcheria. It was impossible ever to familiarize Madame Bianchi, though she had been bred in all respects like her gentle mother, in the same place, and with the same persons. The nonsense of that arch-philosophist Helvétius would be sufficiently confuted by this single example, if such rank folly, contradicted as it is by the experience of every family, needed confutation. She was a beautiful and singular creature, white, with a fine tabby tail, and two or three spots of tabby, always delicately clean; and her wild eyes were bright and green as the Duchess de Cadaval's emerald necklace. Pulcheria did not correspond as she grew up to the promise of her

kittenhood and her name; but she was as fond as her mother was shy and intractable. Their fate was extraordinary as well as mournful. When good old Mrs Wilson died, who used to feed and indulge them, they immediately forsook the house, nor could they be allured to enter it again, though they continued to wander and moan round it, and came for food. After some weeks Madame Bianchi disappeared, and Pulcheria soon afterwards died of a disease endemic at that time among cats.

For a considerable time afterwards, an evil fortune attended all our attempts at re-establishing a Cattery. Ovid disappeared and Virgil died of some miserable distemper. You and your cousin are answerable for these names: the reasons which I could find for them were, in the former case the satisfactory one that the same Ovid might be presumed to be a master in the Art of Love; and in the latter, the probable one that something like Ma-ro might be detected in the said Virgil's notes of courtship.

There was poor Othello: most properly named, for black he was, and jealous undoubtedly he would have been, but he in his kittenship followed Miss Wilbraham into the street, and there in all likelihood came to an untimely end. There was the Zombi – (I leave the Commentators to explain that title, and refer them to my History of Brazil to do it) – his marvellous story was recorded in a letter to Bedford – and after that adventure he vanished. There was Prester John, who turned out not to be of John's gender, and therefore had the name altered to Pope Joan. The Pope I am afraid came to a death of which other Popes have died. I suspect that some poison which the rats had turned out of their holes, proved fatal to their enemy. For some time I feared we were at the end of our Cat-a-logue: but at last Fortune as if to make amends for her late severity sent us two at once – the never-to-be-enough-praised Rumpelstilzchen, and the equally-to-be-admired Hurlyburlybuss.

And 'first for the first of these' as my huge favourite and almost namesake, Robert South, says in his Sermons.

When the Midgeleys went away from the next house, they left this creature to our hospitality, cats being the least movable of all animals because of their strong local predilections; they are indeed in a domesticated state the serfs of the animal creation, and properly attached to the soil. The change was gradually and therefore easily brought about, for he was already acquainted with the children and with me; and having the same precincts to prowl in was hardly sensible of any other difference in his condition than that of obtaining a name; for when he was consigned to us he was an anonymous cat; and I having just related at breakfast with universal applause the story of Rumpelstilzchen from a German tale in Grimm's Collection, gave him that strange and magnisonant appellation; to which upon its being ascertained that he came when a kitten from a bailiff's house, I added the patronymic of Macbum. Such is his history, his character may with most propriety be introduced after the manner of Plutarch's parallels when I shall have given some previous account of his great compeer and rival Hurlyburlybuss – that name also is of Germanic and Grimmish extraction.

Whence Hurlyburlybuss came was a mystery when you departed from the Land of Lakes, and a mystery it long remained. He appeared here, as Mango Gapac did in Peru, and Quetzalcohuatl among the Aztecas, no one knew from whence. He made himself acquainted with all the philofelists of the family – attaching himself more particularly to Mrs Lovell, but he never attempted to enter the house, frequently disappeared for days, and once since my return for so long a time that he was actually believed to be dead and veritably lamented as such. The wonder was whither did he retire at such times – and to whom did he belong – for neither I in my daily walks, nor the children, nor any of the servants ever by any chance saw him anywhere except in our own domain. There was something so mysterious in this, that in old times it might have excited strong suspicion, and he would have been in danger of passing for a Witch in disguise, or a familiar. The mystery however was solved about four weeks ago, when as we were returning from a walk up the Greta, Isabel saw him on his transit across the road and the wall from Shulicrow in a direction towards the Hill. But to this day we are ignorant who has the honour to be his owner in the eye of the law; and the owner is equally ignorant of the high honour in which Hurlyburlybuss is held, of the heroic name which he has obtained, and that his fame has extended far and wide – even unto Norwich in the East, and Escott and Crediton and Kellerton in the West, yea – that with Rumpelstilzchen he has been celebrated in song, by some hitherto undiscovered poet, and that his glory will go down to future generations.

The strong enmity which unhappily subsists between these otherwise gentle and most amiable cats, is not unknown to you. Let it be imputed, as in justice it ought, not to their individual characters (for Cats have characters – and for the benefit of philosophy, as well as felisophy, this truth ought generally to be known) but to the constitution of Cat nature – an original sin, or an original necessity, which may be only another mode of expressing the same thing:

Two stars keep not their motion in one sphere,
Nor can one purlieu brook a double reign
Of Hurlyburlybuss and Rumpelstilzchen.

When you left us, the result of many a fierce conflict was that Hurly remained master of the green and garden, and the whole of the out of door premises, Rumpel always upon the appearance of his victorious enemy retiring into the house as a citadel or sanctuary.

The conqueror was perhaps in part indebted for this superiority to his hardier habits of life, living always in the open air, and providing for himself; while Rumpel (who though born under a bum-bailiff's roof was nevertheless kittened with a silver spoon in his mouth) past his hours in luxurious repose beside the fire, and looked for his meals as punctually as any two-legged member of the family. Yet I believe that the advantage on Hurley's side is in a great degree constitutional also, and that his superior courage arises from a confidence in his superior strength, which as you well know is visible in his make. What Benito and Maria Rosa used to say of my poor Thomaz, that he was *muito hidalgo*, is true of Rumpelstilzchen, his countenance, deportment and behaviour being such that he is truly a gentleman-like Tom-cat. Far be it from me to praise him beyond his deserts – he is not beautiful, the mixture, tabby and white, is not good (except under very favourable combinations) and the tabby is not good of its kind. Nevertheless he is a fine cat, handsome enough for his sex, large, well-made, with good features, and an intelligent countenance, and carrying a splendid tail, which in Cats and Dogs is undoubtedly the seat of honour. His eyes which are soft and expressive are of a hue between chrysolite and emerald. Hurlyburlybuss's are between chrysolite and topaz. Which may be the more esteemed shade for the *olho de gato* I am not lapidary enough to decide. You should ask my Uncle. But both are of the finest water. In all his other features Hurly must yield the palm, and in form also, he has no pretensions to elegance, his size is ordinary and his figure bad: but the character of his face and neck is so masculine, that the Chinese, who use the word bull as synonymous with male, and call a boy a bull-child, might with great propriety denominate him a bull-cat. His make evinces such decided marks of strength and courage that if cat-fighting were as fashionable as cock-fighting, no cat would stand a fairer chance of winning a Welsh main. He would become as famous as the Dog Billy himself, whom I look upon as the most distinguished character that has appeared since Buonaparte.

Some weeks ago Hurlyburlybuss was manifestly emaciated and enfeebled by ill health, and Rumpelstilzchen with great magnanimity made overtures of peace. The whole progress of the treaty was seen from the parlour window. The caution with which Rumpel made his advances, the sullen dignity with which they were received, their mutual uneasiness when Rumpel, after a slow and wary approach, seated himself whisker-to-whisker with his rival, the mutual fear which restrained not only teeth and claws, but even all tones of defiance, the mutual agitation of their tails which, though they did not expand with anger, could not be kept still for suspense, and lastly the manner in which Hurly retreated, like Ajax still keeping his face towards his old antagonist, were worthy to have been represented by that painter who was called the Rafaelle of Cats. The overture I fear was not accepted as generously as it was made; for no sooner had Hurlyburlybuss recovered strength than hostilities were recommenced with greater violence than ever. Rumpel, who had not abused his superiority while he possessed it, had acquired meantime a confidence which made him keep the field. Dreadful were the combats which ensued, as their ears, faces and legs bore witness. Rumpel had a wound which went through one of his feet. The result had been so far in his favour that he no longer seeks to avoid his enemy, and we are often compelled to interfere and separate them. Oh it is awful to hear the 'dreadful note of preparation' with which they prelude their encounters! – the long low growl slowly rises and swells till it becomes a high sharp yowl — and then it is snapt short by a sound which seems as if they were spitting fire and venom at each other. I could half persuade myself that the word felonious is derived from the feline temper as displayed at such times. All means of reconciling them and making them understand how goodly a thing it is for cats to dwell together in peace, and what fools they are to quarrel and tear each other, are in vain. The proceedings of the Society for the Abolition of War are not more utterly ineffectual and hopeless.

All we can do is to act more impartially than the Gods did between Achilles and Hector, and continue to treat both with equal regard.

And thus having brought down these Memoirs of the Cats of Greta Hall to the present day, I commit the precious memorial to your keeping, and I remain

Most dissipated and light-heeled daughter,
Your most diligent and light-hearted father,
Robert Southey
Keswick, 18th June 1824

Incident on East Ninth

JILL DROWER

I leaned my head against the cool metal of the reinforced door. Something was digging into my temple – the spy-hole. I pictured Arnold peeping through from the other side, squinting at me with a cold, cold eye, resentful, gloating, wishing me dead. He loathed me. I realized it the first moment we were introduced. Arnold got me into this. It was all his fault.

It was hot – somewhere in the eighties. This was a smart apartment block in the East Village, but the corridor still looked like it belonged to cell block B at a state pen. It was stifling but I was shaking more than a leaf on a Dutch elm. Was it embarrassment or shock? Every few minutes the elevator would chime and ping out another group of homecomers. They would glance over in my direction and then look away indifferently. What was the matter? Didn't I look weird enough for them? Dishevelled, furtive, I pressed up close to the apartment door in a feeble attempt to conceal myself behind the architrave.

The T-shirt I was wearing was a little tatty, but it was as bright-white as new. It came down just below my navel and it had giant sans serif letters across the chest which spelt out the word 'RELAX'. This was my first night in New York and I was locked out of my friend's apartment. I was telling myself to calm down. Difficult. Apart from the T-shirt, all I was wearing was a pair of gold-hoop earrings.

Arnold's relationship with Laura was entirely platonic. Having shared the apartment for some years they were now as close as brother and sister. Laura was relieved to find a flatmate who accepted her as she was, someone who didn't squabble about petty things like who did the washing-up. Besides, living in New York was a lonely business and Arnold was entertaining company. The problem was, he was jealous of her friends. Maybe he thought that, if she found someone and fell in love, she might want to get married and 'the other man' would boot him out. Whatever it was, Arnold made it his business to frighten away any friends whom she invited in. She had taken to visiting singles bars, and this brought a fairly high number of invitations from her to 'come back to my place for coffee'. Arnold developed what he called his 'spooking-out technique' which, after a couple of evenings, he had down to a fine art. Laura, unsuspecting, would disappear into the kitchen to fix the percolator. Arnold, very friendly, would join the visitor on the sofa and, at a given moment, he would put on this stare and become strangely menacing. When Laura returned with the tray, he was back to being the nice guy and would make a big ceremony of leaving the room tactfully to let them sit alone together on the sofa. After one visit, these poor hopefuls never returned.

I was in New York principally to meet a number of old friends who were now living there but, as this was my first visit to the city, I wanted to see as much of Manhattan as possible in the ten days I had.

'You're welcome to stay at my place, if you like, so long as you don't mind sleeping on the sofa.' I took Laura up on her offer. She lived on East Ninth, somewhere near the bottom of Fifth Avenue and near enough to Washington Square Park for us to go jogging there every morning.

The journey from La Guardia to Laura's apartment had me in a trance. It was all exactly like those cop shows and Scorsese films I'd seen, only much more so. It was all so different from the ribbons of mock Tudor en route from Heathrow or Gatwick. I took it all in: the weatherboard houses, the freeways, the automobiles, the 'last exit to ...' signs and the bluntness of the yellow cab driver who took me from the bus terminal to Laura's place. Like the uninitiated in any major city, I saw the place as a series of clichés. All that was missing was the steam coming out of subway gratings, but I suppose I had the wrong time of year for that. This was summer in the city and fire-hydrant-unlocking time. Firecrackers snapped all around, a constant reminder that July the 4th was only a day away.

Laura was a model host. She took me for brunch and a short walk through the Village. Being an architect, she was able to talk interestingly about the brownstone buildings around. She did warn me briefly about Arnold, saying he was a bit fractious, but no more was said about him that afternoon. Anyway, I reckoned I could manage to soften him up easily enough and that, in no time, we'd be getting along fine.

That first evening a whole group of us ate out in Little Italy to celebrate the reunion of an old gang of friends. I had Conchiglie alla Siciliana which seemed to me the most wonderful dish I had ever tried. We toasted the chef and then drank to absent friends. The man who served us was attentive and gave me a special smile which made him look like a member of the Corleone family. 'I haven't said goodbye to the waiter,' I exclaimed as we were leaving the building. 'He'll live,' said the manageress in the kind of Brooklyn accent I'd kill for if I were an actress. We all laughed and linked arms walking briskly back past the down and outs on the Bowery.

'Do come with us,' said Emil. 'You're only here for a few days.' He wanted me to join them for a late-night showing of *Kiss Me Kate* in 3D. 'No, I'm really too tired, I haven't slept for nineteen hours,' I made my excuses, trying to draw some sympathy. 'I'll see you all tomorrow when the jet lag's worn off.' They accompanied me as far as the junction of Astor Place and Broadway. Laura explained once more how the spare key worked. 'If you get stuck, ask the super.' I looked blank. 'The janitor,' she translated. 'What's a janitor?' I joked in my most pompous English accent.

I let myself in without difficulty and walked over to the window. It was wide open. Just level with the bottom of the frame was a large expanse of flat roofing. At the far end was the ironwork of a fire escape. 'Fire escapes,' I thought. 'Now I know I'm in New York. Cookie, elevator, faucet, super, janitor, I wonder if they have their own word for fire escape too.'

On the sofa was a neat pile of sheets. I managed to assemble it all into some sort of order and struggle into my T-shirt ready for bed. As I lay there half-asleep, I wondered mildly why Laura was so lax about security, but I was too sleepy to get up and close the window. I sank under the cover and within a few seconds I had drifted into sleep.

I woke with a start and lay there for several minutes listening to the whoop-whoop-whoop of police patrol cars and watching the thin curtains billow in the grimy night air.

At some point, I realized I was not alone. The intruder was there somewhere in the room. I stumbled through the darkness towards the door, upsetting a table as I went. I felt something sharp slash my flesh as I groped madly around the wall for a light switch and found it. Then we were looking straight at each other in the lighted room. My attacker, with his vicious penetrating eyes, was standing a few feet away, holding my gaze with his, pinning me to the spot with nothing more than his burning, piercing, hating eyes.

I knew that, if I moved, my assailant would try another slash. We stayed frozen like that for a few moments – musical statues without the music – blood dripping down from the deep gashes in my legs. I had to protect my body from the next attack. Beside me on the floor was a pile of old copies of *Rolling Stone* magazine. Moving quickly, I tried to whip the newsprint in front of me as a shield, but he was far quicker on the draw and cut through the backs of my hands in a trice. He was now taking systematic swipes at any exposed part of me that he could reach. I was no match.

I grappled with the front-door latch and shot through to the hallway. This time Arnold was not quite quick enough. I pulled the door until I heard a gentle click as the latch locked home.

I don't know how long I stood there in that Greenwich Village hallway, half-naked, in a state of trembling indecision.

At last, I crept down to the basement by the back stairs and followed the sound of an early hours news channel reporting preparations for the Independence Day celebration fireworks on the West Side. The janitor looked me slowly up and down, but more down than up.

'Do you happen to have a first-aid box?' I asked meekly. 'And something for me to wear?' He shuffled about and produced a large paint-spattered sheet which I wrapped around me like a toga. After further searching he came up with an old rag, stiff with dried metal polish. After dabbing at the gashes with it for a few moments, I managed to work out that it had once been some kind of undergarment.

'I've been attacked by a cat,' I explained.

'Lady,' he replied, 'you got problems.' He wasn't planning to solve them for me, just commenting. He went back to listening to the broadcast.

'I've also been locked out of apartment number 208. I don't suppose you've got a spare key, have you?'

He dug a credit card out of his wallet and I followed him back up to the flat. He started to work away with the plastic. He seemed amazingly skilled at breaking in and I began to wonder what he did for a living before he was a janitor. Still, this was not the moment to doubt the man whose help I badly needed. My assistant was the silent type, so I did all the talking. 'As soon as the door opens, I'll throw this in.' I waved the polishing-rag undies. 'Don't leave until I've got past him into the bedroom.' I rolled them up tight into a ball and got ready to throw.

The door swung wide open. Arnold was across the other side, eyeing me, quivering in readiness. Ignoring the janitor, he waited for me to make my move. I bowled the brasso ball, medium speed, with a bit of spin. While he was savaging it, I slipped past into Laura's bedroom and shut the door, calling out my thanks to the indifferent janitor. Wasting no time, I took a ladderback chair and tucked it smartly under the door handle.

I switched on the TV. It was tuned to a Spanish language programme. 'Adónde vas? A que no te atreves a besarme?' I flicked the button to the next channel number. Behind me the bedroom-door handle was rattling and jerking. I checked the chair back was still tightly wedged in position, and then settled down to the programme. It was a threesome gameshow. The secretary was called Barbara. She knew far more about husband Bob than wife Connie did. Still, Connie was being very sporting about it; even when it emerged that it was Barbara, not Bob, who had chosen her tenth anniversary present, she laughed ecstatically and applauded her humiliation along with the studio audience.

All this time, Arnold was still pounding on the handle, trying to hurry up the metal fatigue. I turned the volume up to maximum and set my face to the screen. Then suddenly nothing. Silence outside.

I heard the front latch turn and heard Laura's voice.

'Hi, Arnold, how yer been?' She walked in to greet me wearing cardboard glasses, one red side, one green. She stopped in her tracks. 'Looks like you've been having some 3D effects in here.' She looked round at all the furniture in disarray.

Over the next few days Laura did what she could to try to make Arnold see me in a more positive light. These efforts included getting me to give him a bowl of Nine Lives Formula, a plan which went disastrously wrong. Simple tasks like walking to the bathroom or making a cup of coffee were now a nerve-wracking ordeal. 'Try and relax,' Laura would encourage me as I started my journey across the room. 'Are you sure this is a good idea? Couldn't we lock Arnold away just till I go out?' I pleaded. Then I'd hear him scurrying along after me and feel his claws as they found their way through the denim to my tender flesh.

Laura eventually brought in a cat psychiatrist because she was seriously worried about his worsening behaviour. A neighbour had already threatened litigation after Arnold took a swipe one afternoon. 'I'd better do something or, sooner or later, someone is going to take me to court. Suing someone you know is our most popular national pastime. People take classes in it at night school.'

A series of appointments were set up with a very nice Argentinean therapist called Graciela. 'She says I am Arnold's emotional blanket,' Laura confided after one of these consultations. 'And she thinks he's suffering from an abandonment complex.' I felt this was all a very pricey way to find out the obvious, but I kept these thoughts to myself.

The therapist explained what single-cat syndrome was, and suggested that Laura buy Arnold his own little kitten to play with. He was also put on a course of Valium. With half a tablet he was still attacking me. On one whole pill he couldn't quite coordinate enough, so he would just stare at me. In fact, Arnold did a lot of staring over the next few days. At primary school, I can remember a huge portrait of the Queen which hung in the dining-room. I noticed that it didn't matter which table I sat at, her eyes would always be looking directly at me. Having Arnold around was a bit like that, only it wasn't a case of wherever I looked from but whenever I looked. From time to time, it might be two minutes or twenty, I would glance up from my guide book or Manhattan street plan, and there he'd be, eyeballing me. I never saw him blink.

Laura followed all the advice she was given except the bit about buying Arnold his own little kitten. Somehow, she never got around to visiting that pet store on Hudson Street. It would, on reflection, have been a bad idea. Picture Arnold patting and putting the fluffy little thing around the room like an outsize mouse.

This story does have a happy ending (for Arnold at any rate) because, after a few days, I gave up and moved to a hotel. He celebrated his victory by becoming docile and lovable once more. He continued to preside over Laura's spinsterhood, but now with increased confidence.

As for Laura, she carried on her social life outside the flat and rarely invited people back. The offers of a bed to visiting tourist friends ceased after my trip which, for someone living in such a sought-after spot on the globe, must have come as something of a relief. It certainly gave her more time to concentrate on her work and later that year she was promoted, so I suppose there was a happy ending for her too.

'I've landed this incredible job,' she phoned me about a year later. 'It's a complete renovation of an art gallery in SoHo.'

'How's Arnold these days?' I asked.

'Oh, he couldn't be better. He's right by my side, can't you hear him purring?'English philosopher Jeremy

27

Jeremy Bentham's Cat

JOHN BOWRING

Bentham (1748-1832) was a fervent believer in, and chief expounder of, Utilitarian ethics. Here, his friend John Bowring describes one of Bentham's favourite pets.

Bentham was very fond of animals, particularly 'pussies', as he called them, when they had domestic virtues, but he had no particular affection for the common race of cats. He had one, however, of which he used to boast that he had 'made a man of him', and whom he was wont to invite to eat macaroni at his own table. This puss got knighted, and rejoiced in the name of Sir John Langbourne. In his early days he was a frisky, inconsiderate, and, to say the truth, somewhat profligate gentleman; and had, according to the report of his patron, the habit of seducing light and giddy young ladies, of his own race, into the garden of Queen's Square Place: but tired at last, like Solomon, of pleasures and vanities, he became sedate and thoughtful – took to the church, laid down his knightly title, and was installed as the Reverend John Langbourne. He gradually obtained a great reputation for sanctity and learning, and a Doctor's degree was conferred upon him. When I knew him, in his declining days, he bore no other name than the Reverend Doctor John Langbourne: and he was alike conspicuous for his gravity and philosophy. Great respect was invariably shown his reverence: and it was supposed that he was not far off from a mitre, when old age interfered with his hopes and honours. He departed amidst the regrets of his many friends, and was gathered to his fathers, and to eternal rest, in a cemetery in Milton's garden.

The Conscientious Cat

AGNES A. SANDHAM

It was a curious place for a cat – the lonely Hydraulic Mines, on the crest of the Sierra Nevada Mountains in California. Where she came from, no one could tell. My acquaintance with her was made in a singular and altogether startling manner. It was in this wise: I was visiting the mines, and, under the guidance of the superintendent, had just passed over the brow of a great hill crowned with a thick growth of magnificent sugar pines, when suddenly we came upon the Hydraulic Mines – so lonely, so dreary, so utterly uninviting in appearance and situation, that I could not help asking, 'Could anything but a gold–hunting man be induced to live in such a place?'

.'Wait and see,' replied the superintendent as he walked in the direction of a rough shanty used by the miners as a place of shelter.

Just then I was startled at seeing a white cat come dashing toward us at full speed, her tail puffed out to an enormous size, and apparently pursued by a number of men armed with picks and crowbars.

Full of sympathy for the poor cat making such a wild race for her life, I glanced toward the shanty which must be her only refuge. As I did so a dog's head was thrust cautiously out – only the head – and then stopped.

Round the corner of the hut dashed the flying cat, and, before the dog's head could be drawn in, there came a violent collision, and a perfect storm of howls and hisses which marked the meeting of the angry cat and the much astonished dog. In spite of my sympathy, I could not help laughing heartily at this ludicrous collision – and my laugh was echoed by the cruel men who, as I supposed, were chasing poor Pussy with murderous designs. But my laughter was suddenly cut short as I saw what seemed to be the great mountain sliding directly upon me, and, following the example of the cat, I turned and fled for shelter to the hut, while the men redoubled their laughter.

'What under the sun is the matter?' I asked, perplexed alike by the cat, the rushing men, and the moving mountain.

And then, with many jokes and much laughter, the whole matter was explained.

It appears that one cold and stormy night, about a year before my visit to the mines, the men were startled by a pitiful mewing outside the camp. One of the miners, following up the sound of distress, soon returned with a most forlorn and miserable–looking kitten, more dead than alive. How she came to that desolate camp and where she came from was a mystery, but the miners, naturally tender–hearted, and welcoming anything that brought a change in the monotony of their daily life, took pity on the foundling and at once adopted her. Perhaps, too, the sight of such a homebody as a cat, away off in that desolate spot, brought back memories of their boyhood and the old homes far to the east in Maine woods or on New Hampshire hills, and called up, for all of them, a picture of the happy childhood days before the fever of adventure had led them so far from the dear old home in the mad race for gold.

Well, whatever their thoughts, they adopted the cat and made her so warm and comfortable, with plenty of milk to drink and a warm fire to curl before, that Pussy was soon purring away as contentedly as if she had never been a homeless wanderer.

There is no such thing as stopping work in the mines. Day and night the work goes on, and the men are divided into day and night gangs, each of which works for a certain length of time, relieving the other at regular intervals. So it happened that Pussy, dozing before the fire, was aroused by a stir in the room, and glancing up saw the miner who had rescued and cared for her preparing to go out to his work. Determined not to lose sight of her preserver, she jumped up and followed him. When the men arrived at their destination, Pussy at once took up her position near her friend and carefully watched the proceedings.

A hydraulic mine is one in which water is made to take the part of pick and shovel. A tremendous pressure forces the water through a great iron pipe three or four feet in diameter, and sends it in a torrent against the bank of dirt in which the gold is hidden. This mighty stream of water washes away the bank and brings it caving and tumbling down, while it separates the gold from the gravel, and with the occasional assistance of blasting powder does a vast amount of mining work.

It was at one of these hydraulic mines that the fugitive cat had found friends; and as after several visits she lay watching their operations, she seemed to reason it all out in her own mind that as soon as the great dirt bank opposite her showed signs of giving way under the action of the water forced against it, the men would rush for shelter to the shanty nearby, to which, of course, she too would scamper to escape the falling earth. So, reasoned Pussy, if these kind friends of mine are always in danger from these tumbling-down banks, why cannot I, in return for their kindness, watch the dirt banks and give them proper warning?

Now, as you all know, there is nothing a cat dislikes so

much as water; just watch your kitty shake her paws daintily when she steps into a puddle, and see how disgusted she is if a drop of water falls on her nose or back. But this Sierra Nevada pussy was a most conscientious cat. She felt that it was her duty to make some sacrifice for her friends, and so, after thinking it all over, she took her place right on top of the nozzle of the 'monitor' (as the big iron pipe through which the water is forced is called), and here, in spite of occasional and most unwelcome shower baths, she would watch for the first movement of the falling bank, when away she would go like a flash with all the miners at her heels, until they all reached the shelter of the hut. So faithfully did she perform her self-imposed task that, in a little while, the men gave up their precaution of keeping one eye on the dangerous slide and waited for Puss to give the signal. As soon as they saw her spring down from the comfortable bed which the miners had made for her on the monitor, they would all cry, 'The cat, the cat!' and start on a run for the shanty. And it was at just such a moment that I came to the mine and encountered this most conscientious cat leading her friends to safety.

She soon learned also to distinguish between the various phases of hydraulic mining; and when the monitor was being used simply for washing the gold or for general cleaning–up purposes, she knew that there was no danger, and would serenely close her eyes and take a comfortable nap on her cushion, regardless of what was going on around her, until by some strange instinct she knew that the monitor was turned upon the bank again, and was awake and watchful in an instant. Her very colour, too, was a help to her friends, as, being a white cat, she served on dark nights as a guide to the men who came to relieve the gang to which Pussy belonged, and which no consideration would induce her to desert.

Now, it happened that about the time of Pussy's appearance at the mine a very unprepossessing mongrel pup had been left at the camp, as not worth taking away, and so he too was adopted by the kind–hearted miners. But alas! The dog proved as great a coward as the cat was a heroine. His only thought was to look out for number one, and he did that so thoroughly that when he too had learned that a sudden move on the part of the men meant danger, he would scud into the hut in an agony of fear, and, like the dastardly dog he was, retreat into the farthest corner with his tail between his legs. Evidently, when I first made his acquaintance, he had not heard them rushing toward the hut and had thus been caught napping, and hence the collision I had witnessed. He was such a good-for-nothing that the men called him 'Tailings' which also means the refuse gravel and dirt out of which every speck of gold has been taken. And in such awe did he stand of Pussy that, though they took their meals together, Tailings always waited until Pussy had finished before he presumed to take a bite, wagging his tail until the ground was swept clean, and whining meanwhile with hunger and impatience. Once, and once only, he endeavoured to assert himself and take a bite before his betters. Pussy stopped eating, looked the culprit sternly in the eye, and then, slowly lifting her paw, brought it down with a sudden blow exactly in the center of the dog's nose. Tailings gave such a howl that the miners thought the whole mountain was caving in, and rushed out to see what was the matter. Pussy went on calmly finishing her dinner, and Tailings never again presumed to eat at the first table, to rebel against Pussy's rules.

The Black Cat of Killakee

DANIEL COHEN

A building at Killakee in southern Ireland that was used as an arts centre was assailed by a variety of different ghostly phenomena, the worst of which was a monstrous black cat.

The building, called Dower House, was almost in ruins when it was purchased in 1968 by Mrs Margaret O'Brien, an artist and poet, and her husband, Nicholas. The house had been deserted for years, and there was so much renovation work to be done that some of the workmen were actually living on the site during the rebuilding. They were first disturbed by strange sounds and doors that seemed to open mysteriously. But it was the sudden appearance and disappearance of a large black cat that most troubled them.

At first Mrs O'Brien refused to take the stories seriously. 'I thought the whole thing was nonsense,' she said. 'A group of country people sitting alone in an empty house on a lonely hillside at night telling each other stories and frightening themselves. Then I saw the creature myself and I began to understand their fear.'

She described the black cat as being about as big as a medium – sized dog. The first time she came across the creature, it was squatting in the hallway. All of the doors of the house had been locked before the black cat appeared, and they remained locked after it disappeared.

A painter named Tom McAssey, who was helping to decorate the house, had an even more alarming experience. He was working in a room with two other men when suddenly the room, which had been quite warm, became icy cold. The room had been locked, but now the door stood wide open. A 'shadowy figure stood in the darkness beyond,' said McAssey. 'At first I thought someone was playing a joke and I said; 'Come in, I see you.' Then there was a deep sort of guttural growl and the three of us turned and ran in panic. We slammed the heavy door behind us, and I turned and looked back. The door was open again, and a monstrous black cat with red-flecked amber eyes was crouched

there in the half-light. I thought my legs wouldn't take me away from the place. . . . I was really in a bad state.' McAssey also reported seeing a shadowy figure in the hall which said in a deep voice, 'You cannot see me. You don't even know who I am.'

In 1968 Mrs. O'Brien had an exorcism performed in the house, and that seemed to quiet things down for about a year. But in the autumn of 1969, a group of actors who were staying at the arts centre decided – half-seriously – to hold a séance, and after that the disturbances started once again.

Next Mrs O'Brien called in a spirit medium named Sheila St. Clair, who went into a trance and said that she saw the spirits of two women who had helped to serve at Black Masses held by a group of Devil worshippers called the Hell Fire Club in the eighteenth century.

The O'Briens also unearthed some local legends about Thomas 'Black' Whaley, the notorious and depraved member of a rich family in the area who had once joined such a society. Furthermore the legend told of how Whaley and some of his friends had killed a deformed boy just for sport at Dower House. It was said that a small deformed skeleton was unearthed on the grounds of Dower House in 1968. A small metal statue of a devil was also dug up near the house.

There were those who suspected that the whole thing was a publicity stunt for the arts centre, for the press attention certainly helped to attract larger crowds to exhibitions and boost the sale of paintings.

Mrs O'Brien, however, insisted that such was not the case and that the disturbances were more of a problem than an aid to the centre. 'I finally decided to have the house and grounds exorcised once again, and in July 1970 a priest came up from Dublin. Since then we have had very few disturbances, although the priest felt there were still 'emanations' around and we do get the odd bump in the night.'

Cats of my Childhood

MAY EUSTACE

The nostalgic longing for childhood days superimposes itself on everything I write.

> Why do I write,
> What sin to me unknown,
> Dipt me in ink,
> My parents' or my own?

Alexander Pope

Looking back on my yesterdays is to me an exercise in solace and inspiration. No other human experience fills me with such delight. When I reminisce I forget all the cares of the world. I forget that I am getting old. I forget that I am now nearly altogether alone. I forget that I have tax forms to fill in and pension books to sign. I forget all the irritations of the present and enjoy again the old familiar haunts, with the old folks and the animals who first taught me how to live.

> I remember, I remember,
> The house where I was born,
> The little windows where the sun,
> Came peeping in at dawn.

Yes, those were the days. Clearly, as through a looking-glass, I see the old home, the gardens, the paddocks and rivulets. And I see the pathway, too, which leads to the river and the woods carpeted with bluebells, primroses and cowslips. And then – as if I ever could forget – I see my mother and father again.

Mother's long black skirt is trailing in the dust and my father's moustache seems longer and bushier than before. They are speaking in whispers, as if they still have some unfinished business in hand. It was the business of love and sex. Our family was not yet complete.

And, fortunately for us children, our parents were so taken up with each other that they left us very much to our own devices. Within reason we could do what we liked. The same good fortune followed the cats. They were everywhere, males and females together, just living their own lives in their own sweet ways. I know that mother never had a kitten destroyed and there were many of them coming and going in all directions. If I had today's official standards of points I am sure I would have found, amongst them, Rexes and Havanas, Silver Tabbies and British Blues and Bi-coloureds galore.

I was only a small child when the seeds of cat enchantment were sown within me. Not in a namby-pamby way but in a studious and interested fashion, more becoming to an older child. And I repeat again that cats were everywhere. On a sunny day they came out in number, each selecting its very own sheltered and sunny spot. Ostensibly, none of these outdoor cats could claim from us a roof for their heads. We had our own recognized cat dynasty, which included the cat belonging to Rosey, our old housekeeper, and one or two others who scrounged their own kind of living. But we had plenty of surplus rations which we handed out freely to the strays.

But how many of these multi-coloured or self-coloured

cats were really strays? There was one little tabby who always had her afternoon nap on my windowsill. She basked in the sunshine like an oriental goddess. She felt and smelled good. Her ears stood up sharply and she had wisdom written all over her little striped face. She had a cute black nose which seemed to direct her always to the sun. I would not say that she was an over-friendly cat. She did not permit too many familiarities – one or two little rubs, a tickle under her chin, a gentle touch to her little thick tail. No more. She let me know she did not like my overtures and stood up and went away. I thought that an apt name for her would be Winny Silly.

Our next sunbather was the doorstep cat. He was pure black and every inch a male. I was sure of this because I often heard Rosey using bad language towards him; nevertheless, he sat it out though his noxious presence angered the humans. He was quite an agreeable old fellow and permitted me to rub him down and tickle his chin. We called him Steptoe, not after the TV character we know today, but because of his location preference and also after our uncle. He was a very rich farmer and came to Kilkenny once a year. He did not trust anyone to do his buying and selling and when he came down the road on a fair day he had the biggest herd of cattle of all the farmers. He specialized in the Herefordshires and congratulated himself on being a quality breeder. He had only one weakness: he always celebrated a good sale with a good drink. He liked his whiskey neat and always ordered it in doubles. Mother did not seem to mind for she said it was his own money he spent and he could do what he liked with it – his pockets always bulged with £5 and £10 notes. When my father helped him into his cart he just dropped down in the straw like an asphyxiated pig and the pony went along home without any direction, keeping to his own side of the road and negotiating his entrance to the drive carefully.

But Steptoe held onto the step no matter who was

coming and going, so long as it was sunny and warm. You were at liberty to step over him but not to displace him.

The barn cat was a black and white one and the most determined sunbather of the lot. He was not so distinguished-looking as Steptoe. His coat was rather coarse, there were odd smudges of white on his tummy and the tip of his tail was white for a good half-inch. He was domesticated, too, and never objected to having his whiskers pulled. Like the others, whose names were associated with their own selected habitat, we found that Barny was a heaven-ordained name for him. He always hung round the barn and it would appear that he had a special friendship for the little black Kerry cow who was housebound until her calf was born. She was known to wander and had her calves in the most unlikely places. Once she actually gave birth while standing in a stream. Only by the merest fluke was she found in time. In the meantime, if the sun shone, Barny came out to enjoy it and, if the weather was bad, he went into the straw with the cow. Sometimes we did not see him around for a couple of weeks. He did not smell so much of cat as of cow dung.

With regard to smells and scents country folk are more discriminating than those born in towns. The scents of lilacs and roses could never obliterate the smells associated with animals. But Rosey had a town nose, really, and particularly disliked tom cat odour. If she got the slightest whiff she was away for the dog or for her switch.

Then there was the most beautiful of all the cats – the white Persian. I say 'beautiful', but I ought to have said 'could have been beautiful', for her coat was always very dirty. Her lovely fan-like tail was trailed in the dirt too. I am absolutely certain that she had blue eyes which she used to advantage – if ever a cat winked an acknowledgment it was Persi. Her favourite haunt was the stable where we kept the big brown stallion. He was an enormous fellow and generated a special kind of heat which appealed to cats. Persi did not have to cuddle up to him; you could always see the perspiration coming from his body. Though he was a noble beast, full of puissance and fertility, the occasion for him to prove himself never arose.

Besides those named there were also more cats hiding in the hay lofts and it only needed the sun to bring them out. It was interesting to see how the various cats reacted to weather changes. I do not know what Kilkenny weather is like now but I remember that, half a century ago, it was always raining. My mother pointed out that the ever-green grass and the lush vegetation everywhere was the result of the pleasant moist climate. She loved the rain. Once she went on a holiday to her brother in Wembley and she said the weather was too clammy and dry; she longed for the drip, drip, drip, that seemed to be going on forever round our old home. I can remember standing so often in the porch waiting for the sun to shine and my pal and I chanted the popular dirge, 'Rain, rain, go to Spain, and never come back again'. During these wet periods the cats disappeared altogether. All, of course, except our own cats who had managed to sequester themselves in some quiet corners. But no stray cats were allowed the comfort of Rosey's kitchen. She did not keep her hearth so beautifully polished and the surrounding brasses so exquisitely radiant and shining to dazzle the eyes of the strays. This inviting spot was hers and for her little cat alone. Even the house dogs on the payroll were not encouraged to loiter in the comforting glow from the turf fire and the logs.

It was really Nan that set our project in action. Nan was one of the songsters who was with me singing in the rain. She was also one of my best school friends and had a big heart for all cats.

'Where is Winny Silly today?' she asked, seeing the vacant corner.

'Funny you should ask as I was just wondering the same myself. Every time it rains she goes away. Suppose we try to find out where her second home is?' I replied.

'Yes,' said Nan, 'we will run after her next time she comes and decides to leave.'

'And there are others, too, who sit around in the sun for days at a time and as soon as the weather breaks – away they go. It would be fun to find out where they all live.' And there and then we embarked on a project which would establish for all time the true homes of all our visiting felines.

It was quite a few days before we could get our plan started. The weather had been most inviting and we saw all the cats in their sunbathing haunts. I told Nan that mother had prophesied that the low clouds now in the sky meant that rain was on the way. And she was right. Nan had barely arrived when the first drops fell. The first to really get the message was Winny Silly. She was away in a flash with the two of us after her. She jumped over the garden gate like a born athlete, wound her way along the hedge, through the woodside, in and out amongst the trees. We were both out of breath trying to keep up with her. To make matters worse Nan fell down a marshy slope and commenced to cry, 'I think I will go home. We'll never catch her, and I am so tired.'

But I dismissed her complaints and she soon stopped them and came running on with the same zest as she had at the start. We had Winny in sight when she took a sharp turn into the lane leading to the priest's house. We watched her let herself in through the window with such aplomb that we knew she was home. We waited round for a bit and she did not come out. So that was that. Our first query was solved: Winny Silly was the priest's cat. Sunbathing on my windowsill meant nothing to her. She was there because she liked the shelter it afforded her.

She had no love for stray humans. When life suddenly became hard, and the cruel winds of winter buffeted her about, she knew where she could find comfort – on the welcoming knees of the priest's housekeeper. Here food was plentiful and warmth abundant.

Finding Steptoe's domicile took a more exhaustive search. In the first place a few drops of rain were not enough to displace him. We watched him while he crouched miserably against the wall, while the rain lashed all about him.

'Come on Nan,' I whispered, 'I think he has had enough.' Yes. That was so. He was moving. First, he looked appealingly into Rosey's kitchen. The fire was sending out rays of warmth and light which made Steptoe's skin tickle in anticipation. But before he had as much as put a foot forward Rosey was after him like a ton of bricks.

'No stray cats here, please!' said Rosey in a language that Steptoe understood. He walked sulkily away. We wore heavy rain wear and Wellington boots and continued in Steptoe's wake. Once again he took the same route as Winny, but this time he passed the priest's house and went in the direction of the river. It was like a funeral march for, rain or no rain, Steptoe was in no hurry. He stopped several times for a smell of this and that. Then, quite unexpectedly, he stood in front of his own halldoor but this time it was not the usual kind of door – it was a door that one had to jump over and this abode was a houseboat of sorts. There didn't seem to be any welcoming hands coming out to fondle him; nevertheless, he climbed into the cabin, displaying a proprietorial air, and sat himself down. It was evident that this was his real home. No matter how desolate and dreary everything looked in the rain, we were satisfied that this was where Steptoe lived. Later, mother told us that an old fellow known as Joxer had laid claim to the boat after the death of the real owner. He was known to be respectable and did odd jobs for the farmers. He did quite a good bit of fishing, too, and if anyone wanted a nice fresh trout Joxer was their man.

We were very pleased to have found Steptoe's home. Now we had traced back two of our sunbathers. After that I often purloined some of Rosey's cat food for poor Steptoe because I felt he had a lean time on the boat. Miss Winny Silly needed no extra rations for she lived the life of a lady when she was not on our windowsill. She was well fed and well nourished from the generous table of the fat parish priest.

Now for Barny. His conduct was not always predictable. Sometimes for days he disappeared and then we saw him surreptitiously climb through the window of the cow shed. It was certain there was some sort of affinity between the little Kerry cow and him. When we did approach him he was always amiable and we were sure that he was not an abandoned stray. He was never ravenously hungry like Steptoe, so Nan and I agreed that he came from a good home. Yet we had not a single clue. Finding his home would be a hit-or-miss matter. Unlike Winny and Steptoe he was not driven away by the rain. When his sunbathing was disturbed he just went inside and played the waiting game with the little cow. He lay comfortably in the straw as if time did not matter. Nan and I decided that all we could do was wait. Surely this was wise, for by waiting we found out all we wanted to know about Barny. We were coming home from school one day when a little fellow called Tommy Docherty asked us if we would play a game of marbles with him. As we had never before been asked favours from boys, we agreed to do this.

'Hold on a minute,' said Tommy, 'I see Jimmy, our cat, coming home for his dinner.' And at that very moment we looked into the eyes of Cowshed Barny. So that was that, Barny – alias Jimmy – had a good home.

As we walked back Nan and I congratulated ourselves

on establishing the real identity of Cat Number Three – Barny of the old barn – a cat who had fallen in love with our little cow.

The fourth cat, the dirty white Persian, was the most difficult of all to trace, for she never left the stable. When she was not sunbathing on the roof she was inside with the big horse. She really was a homeless stray as she never left our yard and she was the one cat that was never missing. She was always hungry and ate ravenously in a manner more becoming to a waif and stray than to her Persian forebears. I could never catch her. Nan and I saw her several times a day and we decided that, if we could catch her and clean her up, she would gain entry in to any society – and most certainly into Rosey's kitchen. The word 'Persian' was magic.

We told mother of the lovely white cat we saw in the stable and we were sure she was a Persian.

'Persian, indeed,' said mother, 'and how could a Persian cat be turned into a waif or stray?'

So 'Persian, indeed' was our most difficult quarry. To trace her was not going to be easy.

About this time Nan and I started our education proper at the convent school. No more frolics with Tommy Docherty and his kind. Every morning we walked nearly two miles, along footpaths, leafy lanes, through the woods and fields, passing the old church and graveyard, and up the hill to the convent. A little later mother got us our own pony and trap and we took him to school every day. It was very difficult getting permission to tie him up at the back gate and there was one thing we had to promise and that was that we must clean up every evening. The little nun who was in charge of the roses welcomed the good manure we placed so liberally on her rose trees. Driving backwards and forwards to school, with a car full of scholars, was amongst the proudest and happiest experiences of my early school life.

And soon, very soon indeed, there occurred the last and final key to our cat project. Reverend Mother's first address to the assembly included a request for pupils to keep an eye out for her own very special white Persian cat, which had been missing for about a month.

'Did you hear that, Nan?' I whispered. 'Could it possibly be Persi?'

Trembling all over I put my hand up to speak. 'Please, Mother, I think I know where there is a white Persian.'

'Speak up, child,' was her reply but I was not able to speak any louder and I was summoned to the table.

Then everything changed. Suddenly her voice sounded more kindly and the next thing I knew was that I was being sent home with big Alice, the convent cook. Yes, she immediately identified Fluffie, the convent cat. While the chase was on she told mother that she was a very special cat, having been imported (or rather smuggled in) from the home of a viscount in Le Mans – a special gift to Reverend Mother for services rendered to his daughter while boarding in the convent. Then Alice took mother aside and said that, being a female, she was becoming a real annoyance, especially when the male cat population of the town serenaded her all night. It took quite a little while to catch Fluffie as her month's freedom and life as a waif and stray had whetted her appetite for adventure. With the whole of our working staff guarding every exit from the stable, Alice dived headlong under the horse's belly and emerged with a much-bedraggled Fluffie.

Instead of settling down to be the angelic, white-robed creature she used to be, her stay in the outside world had unsettled her. She was no longer content to listen quietly to the angelus bells and the clanking of the rosary beads as the nuns came and went from their devotions. Celibate and happy though her owners might be, Fluffie was now rebellious. The quiet of the convent was shaken. After a serious conference in the community it was decided that Fluffie would have to move on – not as a horse's mate in a dull and depressing stable but as a companion for someone of importance in the town.

When Reverend Mother's wishes were made public the convent bell rang loud and often as hopeful hearts sought ownership of the most important cat in town. From several applicants Fluffie was presented to the mayor, for who better than the first citizen to win such a prize?

But now the real fun started. On the night of arrival Fluffie escaped up the chimney and it looked as if she would be impossible to catch, so the First Lady sent out a series of SOS. The mayor himself was quickly on the scene and, when he looked up the chimney, he was soon blinded by soot that had been displaced by the cat. More and more SOS to civic dignitaries and others. The district nurse outran the doctor and arrived in time to shout: 'Oh, your Lordship! Your poor, dear Lordship! Water, soap, castor oil and brandy! Quick!'

It did not take Ellen, the district nurse, many minutes to get things under control. She cleaned up the mayor, cheered up the mayoress, nipped the wee brandy and went after the cat. By this time Fluffie was in a more agreeable mood and was not so difficult to catch.

'You may take her if you want,' stammered the mayor, 'she is too much for me with my civic duties.'

And so Fluffie became the nurse's cat.

It is so many years ago that I cannot remember all the details but I know that, after her weekly bath, her coat was as white as snow. She was as sweet as she was handsome – and nurse watched carefully over her morals. The occasional tom who picked up her trail ran for his life if ever he saw nurse appear, so there were never any little Fluffies to carry on the name.

And that was how it was in my youth. Cats and everything to do with them were so much fun.

Juno

HARRIET BEECHER STOWE

Harriet Beecher Stowe (1811-96), the American author of
Uncle Tom's Cabin, lived in a property adjoining that of
fellow writer and cat lover, Mark Twain.

The most beautiful and best trained cat I ever knew was named Juno, and was brought up by a lady who was so wise in all that related to the care and management of animals, that she might be quoted as authority on all points of their nurture and breeding; and Juno, carefully trained by such a mistress, was a standing example of the virtues which may be formed in a cat by careful education.

Never was Juno known to be out of place, to take her nap elsewhere than on her own appointed cushion, to be absent at meal-times, or, when the most tempting dainties were in her power, to anticipate the proper time by jumping on the table to help herself.

In all her personal habits Juno was of a neatness unparalleled in cat history. The parlour of her mistress was always of a waxen and spotless cleanness, and Juno would have died sooner than violate its sanctity by any impropriety. She was a skillful mouser, and her sleek, glossy sides were a sufficient refutation of the absurd notion that a cat must be starved into a display of her accomplishments. Every rat, mouse, or ground mole that she caught was brought in and laid at the feet of her mistress for approbation. But on one point her mind was dark. She could never be made to comprehend the great difference between fur and feathers, nor see why her mistress should gravely reprove her when she brought in a bird, and warmly commend when she captured a mouse.

After a while a little dog named Pero, with whom Juno had struck up a friendship, got into the habit of coming to her mistress's apartment at the hours when her modest meals were served, on which occasions Pero thought it would be a good idea to invite himself to make a third. He had a nice little trick of making himself amiable, by sitting up on his haunches, and making little begging gestures with his two fore-paws, which so much pleased his hostess that sometimes he was fed before Juno. Juno observed this in silence for some time; but at last a bright idea struck her, and, gravely rearing up on her haunches, she imitated Pero's gestures with her fore-paws. Of course this carried the day, and secured her position.

Cats are often said to have no heart, – to be attached to places, but incapable of warm personal affection. It was reserved for Juno by her sad end to refute this slander on her race. Her mistress was obliged to leave her quiet home, and go to live in a neighbouring city; so she gave Juno to the good lady who inhabited the other part of the house.

But no attentions or care on the part of her new mistress could banish from Juno's mind the friend she had lost. The neat little parlor where she had spent so many pleasant hours was dismantled and locked up, but Juno would go, day after day, and sit on the ledge of the window-seat, looking in and mewing dolefully. She refused food; and, when too weak to mount on the sill and look in, stretched herself on the ground beneath the window, where she died for love of her mistress, as truly as any lover in an old ballad.

You see by this story the moral that I wish to convey. It is, that watchfulness, kindness, and care will develop a nature in animals such as we little dream of. Love will beget love, regular care and attention will give regular habits and thus domestic pets may be made agreeable and interesting.

Anyone who does not feel an inclination or capacity to take the amount of care and pains necessary for the well-being of an animal ought conscientiously to abstain from having one in charge. A carefully tended pet, whether dog or cat, is a pleasant addition to the family of young people; but a neglected, ill-brought-up, ill-kept one is only an annoyance.

The Cherry Tree

DEREK TANGYE

The fog came down again as we were having lunch, and, by the time we had finished, was clinging around the porch where we were sitting. I mentioned a photograph album at this point which contained photographs of my brother's previous visit; and Jeannie said she knew where it was, that it was in her studio, and it would not take a minute for her to fetch it.

She was away several minutes.

'What have you been doing?' asked my brother on her return. 'Feeding the birds?'

'Always doing that!'

I sensed, however, that she was in a state of excitement; and I could not understand why. Whatever the cause she was not going to disclose it in front of my brother.

I had to wait until we were alone.

'When I left you both,' she then told me, 'I went down the path feeling sad that the fog was thick again. Then I saw something which I could not believe was real.'

'What was it?'

'I saw a little black cat looking like the double of Lama and Oliver ... curled up on the grass at the foot of the cherry tree.'

I reacted in the way that might be expected of me.

53

'I hope you chased it away,' I said.

'It ran away on its own.'

'Good.'

I sensed, however, that there could be trouble between Jeannie and me. There were danger signs. The following morning, for instance, the morning when my brother Colin was to leave for his Guildford home on the Cornish Riviera from Penzance station, there was the first danger sign. She did not wait for me to make her a cup of tea, but she was out of bed and dressed within five minutes. Then, through the bedroom window, I saw her disappear up the lane with a saucer in her hand.

'She's being unfaithful,' I murmured to Ambrose who was curled on the bed beside me.

I could, of course, understand her interest in the cat. If, when living some distance away from any habitation, one has already had two black cats coming uninvited to the door, it is natural to be intrigued by the appearance of yet a third. It was also specially intriguing that the arrivals were always black. When I was a fervent anti-cat person I always acted in friendly fashion towards a black cat, almost as if I was in awe of a black cat. I had this superstitious corner in my nature. The act of a black cat crossing my path gave me encouragement. Any other coloured cat, in those fervent anti-cat days, seemed to me to be vermin.

There had been, besides Lama and Oliver, two other black cats who had sought a home at Minack, but their efforts had failed because their timing was wrong.

The first of these cats was called Felix. He had been abandoned when the farm where he lived was sold, and the farmhouse was left empty. True, a neighbour had agreed to look after him, but the arrangements as far as Felix was concerned were unsatisfactory. Hence he began looking around for another home, and chose Minack as the most suitable.

His method of approach was persistent, aggressive

and, for that matter, heart-rending. We first saw his face eagerly looking through the sitting-room window, and when I opened the door he dashed past me indoors, and came face to face with Lama. He would have pounced on Lama in the manner of a heavyweight boxer on a flyweight if I had not instinctively picked him up and thrown him out.

Since we knew where he came from and the circumstances in which he was being cared for, we decided to return him by driving him there in the car. Ten minutes away by road, five minutes across the fields, we deposited him there at midday. At one o'clock he was back on the window sill, his eager face pressed against the glass.

This situation was repeated several times until we decided we had to act drastically. We discovered the address of the new owner of the farm, contacted him and explained that he had bought a black cat as well as the farm. 'Bring him along to me,' said the man immediately – and that was the last we saw of Felix.

The second black cat began roaming around Minack soon after Oliver had died, and when Ambrose was acclimatizing himself to being on his own. He was a small, compact cat and, in contrast to Felix, timid. For no special reason Jeannie called him Fergus.

I became attached to the sight of him coming prancing up the lane, or passing along the stable meadow, or finding him stalking a mouse in the wood. But he was not domineering like Felix. Fergus seemed content just to stay in the neighbourhood without thrusting his personality upon us. Or perhaps he was watching us, waiting to see whether a home with us, and Ambrose, was possible.

Then came the day I found him curled up in a corner of the Orlyt greenhouse in front of the cottage; and I was so excited that I behaved very clumsily. I shut the greenhouse door and rushed to tell Jeannie. When we returned Fergus was in such terror that he was trying to throw himself through the glass. After that incident he never appeared at Minack again.

There was, however, a happy ending. Margaret and George, the potters who live at the end of the lane, had just lost their old cat. Her basket was still in place in their kitchen when one morning, a few days after the Orlyt greenhouse incident, Fergus walked in through their front door and straight away settled himself in the basket. A wise cat.

We said goodbye to my brother at Penzance station, then drove back home, and when we reached the turn by the gate which leads to Oliver land, Jeannie asked me to stop.

'The saucer, I suppose,' I said grumpily.

'Yes,' she said, getting out of the car, and fetching the saucer.

It hadn't been touched.

'There,' I said, 'you were wasting your time.'

Stray cats the world over are courted, and so I could not blame Jeannie for doing so. There are thousands of stray cats at this very moment who are wandering in the neighbourhood of potential homes, watching the occupants, studying their habits, making up their minds whether such occupants would cater for their requirements to their satisfaction. Cats appear to be loners and many a time you will hear someone, as I used to do, complain that, unlike a dog, a cat is incapable of love; and that it is a selfish, demanding animal which only a fool would pander to.

There is a certain truth in this viewpoint, but I think it is unfair to compare a cat to a dog. I have been a dog person from a child, always will be, but there are circumstances which can make a cat a more suitable companion.

In my case the circumstances concern the change in my attitude towards wildlife since we first came to Minack. In the first years I behaved as I had always been ready to do since, as a teenager, my father gave me my first gun. In those youthful days nothing gave me more pleasure than early morning wanderings, a dog, an old English Sheepdog, in fact, beside me while I kept my gun at the ready to shoot any game bird or rabbit on sight. Rough shooting, as it is called, had almost a poetic quality in its pleasure for me. I was a hunter. Killing provided no sense of guilt.

Then slowly, like an ivy creeping up a building, I began at Minack to become aware of the wonder of life in the countryside, and of its struggle to survive; and when, one hard winter, I heard on the other side of the valley the frenetic gunshots of men shooting, the barks of dogs being urged on to retrieve the ducks, the plovers, the snipe which had been killed or half-killed, I knew I no longer subscribed to the attitude of my youth.

As often happens when there is such a change in the attitude of a person's beliefs, there is always a chance he might go to the other extreme. I have not done that. I could never condone, for instance, a politically motivated animal rights group; or accept that fox hunting is worse than gin trapping. I just do not intend to kill. Nor do I wish to disturb wildlife in its natural habitation. I want pheasants to roam around our land without fear, and birds to nest without disturbance, and badgers to be free of Ministry of Agriculture persecution. It means, too, that a dog is out of place at Minack. I would never be able to give it the free run, the free chase, the free barking, that I would have done if I had been at Minack in my youth.

A cat, I find therefore, is an easier companion than a dog. A cat's sense of independence also enables oneself to be independent. A cat can amuse itself on its own and, if it feels like a walk, off it will go. A dog, of course, will demonstrate its love to someone much more obviously than a cat, but then a dog will wag its tail at anyone who pays it attention. A cat will not do that. A cat, on most

occasions, will remain aloof; and this aloofness, curiously, often maddens those very people who profess to adore cats. Such people, with their baby-language noises as they try to coax a cat to take notice of them, are infuriated with the cat which ignores them.

We have been fortunate in that we have never had a cat which caught birds as a pastime; and yet, if I wish to be fair, I do not condemn cats for being bird catchers. I look upon their cats as another example of nature's way of maintaining the balance of nature. There is, after all, continuous warfare in the world of nature, and cats catching birds is part of it.

Nonetheless, I am thankful that our cats have never shown signs of wishing to catch birds; and this thankfulness has always made me hesitate to welcome any new cat arrival at Minack. I would not be able to tolerate such a cat after the peaceful times of Monty, Lama, Oliver and Ambrose.

There was no sign of the cherry tree cat that day, and no sign of it the following day.

'It's returned to wherever it came from,' I said to Jeannie, 'and a good thing too.'

I had no wish for Ambrose's life to be disturbed.

On the Wednesday, however, I went into the hut where once we used to force, by paraffin heat, daffodil buds into full bloom, and I made a disturbing discovery. The hut, among other uses, had become a cat's kitchen. It was here that Jeannie would painstakingly, on a discarded calor-gas stove, boil the coley for Ambrose. The coley came in 10 lb frozen slabs, and Jeannie, the night before, would lay the slab out to de-freeze.

On the Tuesday evening she had laid out such a slab – but when, on the Wednesday, I had gone into the hut I found a part of the still frozen slab gnawed away. The hut door was shut, but there was a small gap between door and floor level. Something had got through it. What?

I said to Jeannie that it must have been a rat, but we never had previous evidence of a rat. The very mention of such a possibility provoked Jeannie into making an extravagant outburst on behalf of the cherry tree cat.

'It was a starving cat that did that,' she said, with all the conviction of a besotted cat lover. 'Only a starving cat would have clawed at frozen fish!'

'How could it have got there? The door was shut.'

'But there was the gap at the bottom, you silly. The cat is a small one, almost a kitten perhaps, and it could easily have got through such a gap.'

I have never tried to pursue my own point of view when Jeannie is in a cat mood. Wise for me to keep silent.

Thursday was a beautiful sunny day, and we got up leisurely, and I said to Jeannie that we should not waste such a lovely day on work, and that we should relax. It is this pure joy of being free to choose the pattern of a day that makes one a millionaire in real terms. No question of what deal to do next, no question of how to spend money to boost one's ego, just the question of whether to take the donkeys first for a walk, or to take Ambrose.

Then, when such pleasurable duties have been decided upon, then completed, there is the question, keeping a sense of guilt always out of sight, as to what to have for lunch – and where.

On this Thursday, Jeannie, because it was like a summer day in October, decided to have our lunch, consisting of Brie from Paxton and Whitfield, on the bridge. We were sitting there, enjoying ourselves, gossiping, making remarks that strangers to us would not understand, when suddenly I saw the cherry tree cat for the first time.

Surrounding Jeannie's studio, which was several yards below where we were sitting, is a high stone wall, high enough to hide the studio from sight. It was on the top of this high wall that I first saw a little black head, then a thin little black body.

'The cat's back!' I called out loudly, loud enough to scare it and make it disappear.

There had been such excitement in the tone of my voice that Jeannie jumped to the conclusion I was pleased to have seen it.

'A little black cat at Minack again! You are pleased, aren't you?'

'No,' I replied, recovering my composure, 'it's going to be a nuisance hovering around, and anyhow where has it come from? It must have come from somewhere.'

My irritation, I have to admit, was superficial only. I was intrigued. I was not, however, going to give Jeannie any encouragement.

'I wonder where it has been since I saw it on Sunday.'

'It is possible,' I said, 'that it is one of Walter's or it belongs to Tregurnow, and it's just a wandering cat.'

Walter Grose, a Pied Piper of cats, had a collection of them at the farm at the top of the lane. Tregurnow was further away, and also had a number of cats.

'Walter,' said Jeannie, 'has never had a black cat.'

'Anyhow,' I said, and felt relieved as I spoke, 'it shows no sign of wishing to be friendly. It is only a shadow at the moment, and long may it remain so.'

Jeannie was silent. Then she said: 'I have a hunch that Cherry is not always going to be a shadow.'

'So you've christened it already.'

'Cherry is the right name for her, finding her under the cherry tree.'

'So it is a her?'

'I'm sure. Small cats are usually female.'

There was no sign of the cat during the rest of the day, no sign of it the following morning, and Jeannie kept wondering where it could have been hiding. In the afternoon, however, she had a pleasant surprise. She had decided to take to Ambrose a saucer of milk in which she had mixed a raw egg, a favourite concoction of his; and as during the day, when he was not hunting, he was usually curled up in the hay which we kept for the donkeys in the Orlyt, she carried it down to him there. Instead of being curled in the hay, however, he was at the far bottom end of the Orlyt staring intently at something. She walked along to him and found, to her astonishment, the cherry tree cat curled up in a round ball, sound asleep, and only a few feet from him.

'Ambrose was absolutely calm,' she told me later, 'but when she woke up and saw me, she bolted. Ambrose didn't chase her. That's a good sign, isn't it?'

Jeannie knew very well that my main objection to any cat infiltration was the question of Ambrose's reaction to it. My own form of loyalty.

'And where did she go?'

'No idea. Completely disappeared.'

'I refuse to believe that Ambrose would ever enjoy the company of another cat.'

'But he didn't chase her, I tell you.'

I guessed that Jeannie had now decided to carry out a secret wooing campaign; saucers containing an assortment of delicacies would be placed at strategic points around Minack. The game would amuse her. She had done it before. I remember when Oliver was hovering in the neighbourhood she left a saucer containing sliced roast chicken halfway up the lane. I happened to look down that way a little later and saw a fox at the saucer, an astonished fox. I spent the Saturday morning of that week fiddling with my brush cutter. The brush cutter is like an outdoor vacuum cleaner, just as important, even more so because, although you can manually dust and clean a house, it is quite impossible to keep cliff meadows manually in trim. The brush cutter is an instrument you sling over your shoulders, has a six-foot-long frame with a circular blade at the end of it. At this time of year, early autumn, it is my special companion. I use it to cut away the undergrowth of our numerous small meadows in readiness for the February daffodil season. Unfortunately my brush cutter would not operate properly. I had bought an early model and it was now tired. I would have to get a new one, I realized.

After lunch, when Jeannie told me she was going for a walk with Fred and Merlin on Oliver land, I said I would have a Churchill. This meant a rest. Churchill was always in favour of a rest after lunch.

I lay down on our bed, and ruminated. Such a rumination can cover a multitude of subjects in quick succession. A long-ago memory can merge into a present-day conflict I might be having with someone who had part control of my future. A flash, no logical reason for it, recalls a time when I stayed for a month in 956 Sacramento Street, San Francisco, then suddenly comes the recall of the occasion when, preparing the ground for early potatoes, the rotovator upset and one of the spikes pierced my foot. I was lying on the same bed as on that first night we stayed at Minack, rain dripping through the roof and Monty, companion on the journey in the Land Rover from Mortlake, beside us. Suddenly I was aware of a whisper noise on the carpet beside me. I looked down and there was the cherry tree cat.

The sight of her had an effect on me. It suggested that she was more than just a cat wandering around in the hope of food, and that she was indeed a cat who was looking for a home. Hence, when next I saw Jeannie, my attitude was a different one. I said to her we had a moral duty to perform. Somebody, I said, must have lost the little cat and would be searching for her at this very moment. Instead of amusing ourselves by thinking she might be another Minack cat, we had to take steps to see if we could find out who might have lost her.

After her inspection of the bedroom she kept out of sight for a couple of days, and we thought she had possibly left the neighbourhood. Perhaps she had just been making use of us, a pause in a journey. But the following Monday Jeannie, still leaving saucers around, suddenly saw her at a saucer opposite the water butt at the corner of the cottage. Jeannie had placed the saucer of temptation in the miniature bed of a rockery; and there, to Jeannie's delight around eight in the morning, she saw the cherry tree cat gulping its contents.

Jeannie left her at the saucer, and came back to tell me what she had seen. Then we both went out to have a look.

There was no cat; and there appeared to be no saucer.

'Look,' said Jeannie, who had bent down, 'she's covered it up! She's covered it up with old grass, like a wild animal hiding its prey.'

'Perhaps that's the explanation,' I said. 'Perhaps she is a wild cat, just as Lama was wild when she first appeared.'

We did not see her again that day until evening time when Jeannie caught sight of her on the path, and promptly filled another saucer; she placed it in the same place as the morning saucer. The incident was repeated. The cat soon came to consume its contents, left a little, and covered it up again with old grass. She was very nervous and, when she caught sight of us, she immediately ran away. A pity, because we were harmless. It was Ambrose she had to be scared of.

The first public confrontation with Ambrose came two mornings later. There may have been a previous confrontation, perhaps a meeting during the night, but this we did not know. The public confrontation, however, was horrific.

Ambrose came serenely out of the porch after a breakfast of coley, strolled confidently past the water butt at the corner of the cottage ... and saw her. He arched his back, growled, spat, then, when the lady saw him and fled, he raced after her. She fled up the path to the clothes line – the clothes line with the most beautiful view in the country, looking across Mount's Bay and with sea breezes drying the clothes – she fled towards it, and seconds later there were such screams that I thought Ambrose was killing her. I followed the two of them and found the lady high up on a privet bush, looking down upon a furious Ambrose.

The incident made me determined to get rid of her.

'Impossible for her to stay around here another day,' I said firmly to Jeannie. 'I just won't tolerate Ambrose being upset.'

'I don't want him upset either.'

'All right then, we are both agreed . But don't feed that cat again.'

'I will,' replied Jeannie defiantly.

'Absurd, quarrelling over an unknown cat.'

Our collision of views did not last long. We compromised. The cherry tree cat would continue to be fed.

The search for her origin would immediately begin.

Calvin, the Cat

CHARLES DUDLEY WARNER

Calvin is dead. His life, long to him, but short for the rest of us, was not marked by startling adventures, but his character was so uncommon and his qualities were so worthy of imitation that I have been asked by those who personally knew him to set down my recollections of his career.

His origin and ancestry were shrouded in mystery; even his age was a matter of pure conjecture. Although he was of the Maltese race, I have reason to suppose that he was American by birth as he certainly was in sympathy. Calvin was given to me eight years ago by Mrs Stowe, but she knew nothing of his age or origin. He walked into her house one day out of the great unknown and became at once at home, as if he had been always a friend of the family. He appeared to have artistic and literary tastes, and it was as if he had enquired at the door if that was the residence of the author of *Uncle Tom's Cabin* and, upon being assured that it was, had decided to dwell there. This is, of course, fanciful, for his antecedents were wholly unknown, but in his time he could hardly have been in any household where he would not have heard *Uncle Tom's Cabin* talked about.

When he came to Mrs Stowe, he was as large as he ever was, and apparently as old as he ever became. Yet there was in him no appearance of age; he was in the happy maturity of all his powers and you would rather have said, in that maturity, he had found the secret of perpetual youth. And it was as difficult to believe that he would ever be aged as it was to imagine that he had ever been in immature youth. There was in him a mysterious perpetuity.

After some years, when Mrs Stowe made her winter home in Florida, Calvin came to live with us. From the first moment, he fell into the ways of the house and assumed a recognized position in the family – I say recognized, because after he became known he was always enquired for by visitors, and in the letters from other members of the family he always received a message. Although the least obtrusive of beings, his individuality always made itself felt.

His personal appearance had much to do with this, for he was of royal mould and had an air of high breeding. He was large, but he had nothing of the fat grossness of the celebrated Angora family; though powerful, he was exquisitely proportioned and as graceful in every movement as a young leopard. When he stood up to open a door – he opened all the doors with old-fashioned latches – he was portentously tall, and when he stretched on the rug before the fire he seemed too long for this world – as indeed he was. His coat was the finest and softest I have ever seen, a shade of quiet Maltese; and from his throat downwards, underneath, to the white tips of his feet, he wore the whitest and most delicate ermine; and no person was ever more fastidiously neat. In his finely formed head you saw something of his aristocratic character; the ears were small and cleanly cut, there was a tinge of pink in the nostrils, his face was handsome and the expression of his countenance exceedingly intelligent – I should call it even a sweet expression if the term were not inconsistent with his look of alertness and sagacity.

It is difficult to convey a just idea of his gaiety in connection with his dignity and gravity, which his name expressed. As we know nothing of his family, of course it will be understood that Calvin was his Christian name. He had times of relaxation into utter playfulness, delighting in a ball of yarn, catching sportively at stray ribbons when his mistress was at her toilet, and pursuing his own tail, with hilarity, for lack of anything better. He could amuse himself by the hour, and he did not care for children; perhaps something in his past was present to his memory. He had absolutely no bad habits, and his disposition was perfect. I never saw him exactly angry, though I have seen his tail grow to an enormous size when a strange cat appeared upon his lawn. He disliked cats, evidently regarding them as feline and treacherous, and he had no association with them. Occasionally there would be heard a night concert in the shrubbery. Calvin would ask to have the door opened, and then you would hear a rush and a 'pestzt', and the concert would explode, and Calvin would quietly come in and resume his seat on the hearth. There was no trace of anger in his manner, but he wouldn't have any of that about the house.

He had the rare virtue of magnanimity. Although he had fixed notions about his own rights, and extraordinary persistency in getting them, he never showed temper at a repulse; he simply and firmly persisted till he had what he wanted. His diet was one point; his idea was that of the scholars about dictionaries – to 'get the best'. He knew as well as anyone what was in the house, and would refuse beef if turkey was to be had; and if there were oysters, he would wait over the turkey to see if the oysters would not be forthcoming. And yet he was not a gross gourmand; he would eat bread if he saw me eating it, and thought he was not being imposed on. His habits of feeding, also, were refined; he never used a knife, and he would put up his hand and draw the fork down to his mouth as gracefully as a grown person. Unless necessity compelled, he would not eat in the kitchen, but insisted upon his meals in the dining-room, and would wait patiently, unless a stranger were present; and then he was sure to importune the visitor, hoping that the latter was ignorant of the rule of the house, and would give him something. They used to say that he preferred as his tablecloth on the floor a certain well-known Church journal; but this was said by an Episcopalian.

So far as I know, he had no religious prejudices, except that he did not like the association with Romanists. He tolerated the servants, because they belonged to the house, and would sometimes linger by the kitchen stove; but the moment visitors came in he arose, opened the door and marched into the drawing-room. Yet he enjoyed the company of his equals, and never withdrew, no matter how many callers – whom he recognized as of his society – might come into the drawing-room. Calvin was fond of company, but he wanted to choose it; and I have no doubt that his was an aristocratic fastidiousness rather than one of faith. It is so with most people.

The intelligence of Calvin was something phenomenal, in his rank of life. He established a method of communicating his wants, and even some of his sentiments; and he could help himself in many things. There was a furnace register in a retired room, where he used to go when he wished to be alone, that he always opened when he desired more heat; but never shut it, any more than he shut the door after himself. He could do almost everything but speak; and you would declare sometimes that you could see a pathetic longing to do that in his intelligent face. I have no desire to overdraw his qualities but, if there was one thing in him more noticeable than another, it was his fondness for nature. He could content himself for hours at a low window, looking into the ravine and at the great trees, noting the smallest stir there; he delighted, above all things, to accompany me walking about the garden, hearing the birds, getting the smell of the fresh earth, and rejoicing in the sunshine. He followed me and gambolled like a dog, rolling over on the turf and exhibiting his delight in a hundred ways. If I worked, he sat and watched me, or looked off over the bank and kept his ear open to the twitter in the cherry trees. When it stormed, he was sure to sit at the windows, keenly watching the rain or the snow, glancing up and down at its falling; and a winter tempest always delighted him.

I think he was genuinely fond of birds but, so far as I know, he usually confined himself to one a day; he never killed, as some sportsmen do, for the sake of killing, but only as civilized people do – from necessity. He was intimate with the flying-squirrels who dwelt in the chestnut tree – too intimate, for almost every day in the summer he would bring in one, until he nearly discouraged them. He was, indeed, a superb hunter, and would have been a devastating one if his bump of destructiveness had not been offset by a bump of moderation. There was very little of the brutality of the lower animals about him; I don't think he enjoyed rats for themselves, but he knew his business and, for the first few months of his residence with us, waged an awful campaign against the horde and, after that, his simple presence was sufficient to deter them from coming on the premises. Mice amused him, but he usually considered them too small game to be taken seriously; I have seen him play for an hour with a mouse and then let him go with a royal condescension. In this whole matter of 'getting a living', Calvin was a great contrast to the rapacity of the age in which he lived.

I hesitate to speak of his capacity for friendship and the affectionateness of his nature, for I know from his own reserve that he would not care to have it much talked about. We understood each other perfectly, but we never made any fuss about it; when I spoke his name and snapped my fingers, he came to me; when I returned home at night, he was pretty sure to be waiting for me near the gate, and would rise and saunter along the walk, as if his being there were purely accidental – so shy was he commonly of showing feeling; and when I opened the door he never rushed in, like a cat, but loitered and lounged, as if he had had no intention of going in, but would condescend to. And yet, the fact was, he knew dinner was ready, and he was bound to be there. He kept the run of dinner-time. It happened sometimes, during our absence in the summer, that dinner would be early, and Calvin, walking about the grounds, missed it and came in late. But he never made a mistake the second day. There was one thing he never did – he never rushed through an open doorway. He never forgot his dignity. If he had asked to have the door opened, and was eager to go out, he always went deliberately; I can see him now, standing on the sill, looking about at the sky as if he was thinking whether it were worth while to take an umbrella, until he was near having his tail shut in.

His friendship was rather constant than demonstrative. When we returned from an absence of nearly two years Calvin welcomed us with evident pleasure, but showed his satisfaction rather by tranquil happiness than by fuming about. He had the faculty of making us glad to get home. It was his constancy that was so attractive. He liked companionship, but he wouldn't be petted, or fussed over, or sit in anyone's lap a moment; he always extricated himself from such familiarity with dignity and with no show of temper. If there was any petting to be done, however, he chose to do it. Often he would sit looking at me and then, moved by a delicate affection, come and pull at my coat and sleeve until he could touch my face with his nose, and then go away contented. He had a habit of coming to my study in the morning sitting quietly by my side or on the table for hours, watching the pen run over the paper, occasionally swinging his tail round for a blotter and then going to sleep among the papers by the inkstand. Or, more rarely, he would watch the writing from a perch on my shoulder. Writing always interested him and, until he understood it, he wanted to hold the pen.

He always held himself in a kind of reserve with his friend, as if he had said, 'Let us respect our personality and not make a "mess" of friendship.' He saw, with Emerson, the risk of degrading it to trivial conveniency. 'Why insist on rash personal relations with your friends. Leave this touching and clanging.' Yet I would not give an unfair notion of his aloofness, his fine sense of the sacredness of the me and the not-me. And, at the risk of not being believed, I will relate an incident which was often repeated. Calvin had the practice of passing a portion of the night in the contemplation of its beauties and would come into our chamber over the roof of the conservatory through the open window, summer and winter, and go to sleep at the foot of my bed. He would do this always exactly in this way; he never was content to stay in the chamber if we compelled him to go upstairs and through the door. He had the obstinacy of General Grant. But this is by the way. In the morning, he performed his toilet and went down to breakfast with the rest of the family. Now, when the mistress was absent from home, and at no other time, Calvin would come in the morning, when the bell rang, to the head of the bed, put up his feet and look into my face, follow me about when I rose, 'assist' at the dressing, and in many purring ways show his fondness, as if he had plainly said, 'I know that she has gone away, but I am here.' Such was Calvin in rare moments.

He had his limitations. Whatever passion he had for nature, he had no conception of art. There was sent to him once a fine and very expressive cat's head in bronze,

by Frémiet. I placed it on the floor. He regarded it intently, approached it cautiously and crouchingly, touched it with his nose, perceived the fraud, turned away abruptly and never would notice it afterwards.

On the whole, his life was not only a successful one, but a happy one. He never had but one fear, so far as I know; he had a mortal and a reasonable terror of plumbers. He would never stay in the house when they were here. No coaxing could quiet him. Of course, he didn't share our fear about their charges, but he must have had some dreadful experience with them in that portion of his life which is unknown to us. A plumber was to him the devil, and I have no doubt that, in his scheme, plumbers were foreordained to do him mischief.

In speaking of his worth, it has never occurred to me to estimate Calvin by the worldly standard. I know that it is customary now, when anyone dies, to ask how much he was worth, and that no obituary in the newspapers is considered complete without such an estimate. The plumbers in our house were one day overheard to say that, 'They say that she says that he says that he wouldn't take $100 for him.' It is unnecessary to say that I never made such a remark, and that, so far as Calvin was concerned, there was no purchase in money.

As I look back upon it, Calvin's life seems to me a fortunate one, for it was natural and unforced. He ate when he was hungry, slept when he was sleepy, and enjoyed existence to the very tips of his toes and the end of his expressive and slow-moving tail. He delighted to roam about the garden, and stroll among the trees, and to lie on the green grass and luxuriate in all the sweet influences of summer. You could never accuse him of idleness, and yet he knew the secret of repose. The poet who wrote so prettily of him that his little life was rounded with a sleep, understated his felicity; it was rounded with a good many. His conscience never seemed to interfere with his slumbers. In fact, he had good habits and a contented mind. I can see him now walk in at the study door, sit down by my chair, bring his tail artistically about his feet, and look up at me with unspeakable happiness in his handsome face.

I often thought that he felt the dumb limitation which denied him the power of language. But since he was denied speech, he scorned the inarticulate mouthings of the lower animals. The vulgar mewing and yowling of the cat species was beneath him; he sometimes uttered a sort of articulate and well-bred ejaculation, when he wished to call attention to something that he considered remarkable, or to some want of his, but he never went whining about. He would sit for hours at a closed window, when he desired to enter, without a murmur, and when it was opened he never admitted that he had been impatient by 'bolting' in. Though speech he had not, and the unpleasant kind of utterance given to his race he would not use, he had a mighty power of purr to express his measureless content with congenial society. There was in him a musical organ with stops of varied power and expression, upon which I have no doubt he could have performed Scarlatti's celebrated cat's fugue.

Whether Calvin died of old age, or was carried off by one of the diseases incident to youth, it is impossible to say; for his departure was as quiet as his advent was mysterious. I only know that he appeared to us in the world in his perfect stature and beauty, and that after a time, like Lohengrin, he withdrew. In his illness there was nothing more to be regretted than in all his blameless life. I suppose there never was an illness that had more dignity and sweetness and resignation in it. It came on gradually, in a kind of listlessness and want of appetite. An alarming symptom was his preference for the warmth of a furnace register to the lively sparkle of the open wood fire. Whatever pain he suffered, he bore it in silence, and seemed only anxious not to obtrude his malady. We tempted him with the delicacies of the season, but it soon became impossible for him to eat, and for two weeks he ate or drank scarcely anything. Sometimes he made an effort to take something, but it was evident that he made the effort to please us. The neighbours – and I am convinced that the advice of neighbours is never good for anything – suggested catnip. He wouldn't even smell it. We had the attendance of an amateur practitioner of medicine, whose real office was the cure of souls, but nothing touched his case. He took what was offered, but it was with the air of one to whom the time for pellets was passed. He sat or lay day after day almost motionless, never once making a display of those vulgar convulsions or contortions of pain which are so disagreeable to society. His favourite place was on the brightest spot of a Smyrna rug by the conservatory, where the sunlight fell and he could hear the fountain play. If we went to him and exhibited our interest in his condition, he always purred in recognition of our sympathy. And when I spoke his name, he looked up with an expression that said, 'I understand it, old fellow, but it's no use.' He was to all who came to visit him a model of calmness and patience in affliction.

I was absent from home at the last, but heard by daily postal card of his failing condition; and never again saw him alive. One sunny morning he rose from his rug, went into the conservatory (he was very thin then), walked around it deliberately, looking at all the plants he knew, and then went to the bay-window in the dining-room and stood a long time looking out upon the little field, now brown and sere, and towards the garden where perhaps the happiest hours of his life had been spent. It was a last look. He turned and walked away, laid himself down upon the bright spot in the rug, and quietly died.

It is not too much to say that a little shock went through the neighbourhood when it was known that Calvin was dead, so marked was his individuality; and his friends, one after another, came in to see him. There was no sentimental nonsense about his obsequies; it was felt that any parade would have been distasteful to him. John, who acted as undertaker, prepared a candle-box for him, and I believe assumed a professional decorum; but there may have been the usual levity underneath, for I heard that he remarked in the kitchen that it was the 'driest wake he ever attended'. Everybody, however, felt a fondness for Calvin and regarded him with a certain respect. Between him and Bertha there existed a great friendship, and she apprehended his nature; she used to say that sometimes she was afraid of him, he looked at her so intelligently; she was never certain that he was what he appeared to be.

When I returned, they had laid Calvin on a table in an upper chamber by an open window. It was February. He reposed in a candle-box, lined about the edge with evergreen, and at his head stood a little wine glass with flowers. He lay with his head tucked down in his arms – a favourite position of his before the fire – as if asleep in the comfort of his soft and exquisite fur. It was the involuntary exclamation of those who saw him, 'How natural he looks!' As for myself, I said nothing. John buried him under the twin hawthorn trees – one white and the other pink – in a spot where Calvin was fond of lying and listening to the hum of summer insects and the twitter of birds.

Perhaps I have failed to make appear the individuality of character that was so evident to those who knew him. At any rate, I have set down nothing concerning him but the literal truth. He was always a mystery. I did not know whence he came; I do not know whither he has gone. I would not weave one spray of falsehood in the wreath I lay upon his grave.

Cats that Swam and Cycled

N. TEULON PORTER

I have had two cats who have led dogs' lives and were both of them constant and willing swimmers. They went for long walks in straight lines across country in a way which is more doglike than catlike. Dogs and wolves hunt as much in the open as in undergrowth, and are accustomed to hunting singly or in packs, running in straight lines, without possibility of refuge or cover, while cats skulk and stalk, and are never really quite at ease unless they are sitting under something, even if it is only a chair or a table. They make no prolonged physical efforts like dogs, though capable of enormous short lived energy output. Take a cat into the middle of a large meadow and she will wail and be filled with fear. If she can see even a rail fence and get under it she is comparatively relieved and will sit up and take stock quietly of the situation. So Tom, in my boyhood, and William twenty years later, lived more, I think, against their true nature by going long steady walks with me than by taking to the water. They were never so happy as when tramping, though they had always a tendency to make a gallop of the last twenty yards to reach any bit of cover or eminence they might see. A molehill was big enough to sit on a moment or a tuft of heather or rushes to crouch beside and regain that composure which I had not noticed they had missed until they regained it by some such means.

They both of them began life with me as kittens and were both short haired. Tom, the first, learned to swim by leaping short across the quiet pools of little mountain streams in his efforts to follow me on our walks. Having flopped in he swam out, and the third time, finding the stream was too broad to jump with ease, he yowled once or twice and then, excitedly and with shocking technique, swam across and was made much of at the other side. After that all hesitation seemed to go and he would always sooner swim than jump, except on very cold or windy days, when sometimes he would run two or three hundred yards along the river to find a good jumping–place sooner than swim, and then gallop after me shouting all the way. This fellow often, after having had to run very hard before he could catch me up, would make a running jump and climb up my stolid unheeding back as he caught me up, and spread himself over my shoulder and tap my ear violently with a soft paw as if correcting me for not waiting. After a hundred yards or two he would get down. He slept in a little wooden kennel nailed on the outside of the stable wall, and, I think, never saw the inside of a house. Often if I sat down beside the water, he would swim or wade about and even take trips of twenty yards or so to the far side, seeking fun and mischief. Neither of these cats ever learned to catch fish by clawing them out from the bank.

William was born in Cambridge and from a very early age rode on my shoulder wherever I went. He kept all my lectures with me and stayed absolutely still when he was on my shoulder, and I taught him not to accept advances from my bench neighbours. He went off shopping with me on my bicycle. He was hardly ever off my shoulder except at home over the fire. He always accompanied me on the river in canoes and punts, generally sitting on the prow – a very excited little figurehead – or, when we met other boats with dogs in them, very stern and still and forbidding. As no occasion arose for him to go into the water, as in Tom's case, I introduced him to it gently. First of all I took him in my hands quietly, with all his four legs hanging over, and lowered him so steadily into still water that finally he floated free of my hand with most of his back still dry and most of the air still in his fur underneath, and he forthwith swam. He climbed out on the bank near by looking very surprised but not at all frightened. Next time we did it, he made no more fuss than the first time, and it was not long before he took to the water for his own pleasure.

This cat went very many hundreds of miles with me on my pedal cycle through the wilder parts of England, riding like a limp sandbag on shoulder and sleeping with me in my little tent every night. In hot weather he felt the heat very much, and, with open mouth and scarlet tongue flapping out, panted like a little motor car into my left ear. And then sometimes, when he saw water near by, he would make as if to get down, and I would stop awhile and let him swim.

On entering a wayside pub, he would go right through the house walking straight up on high legs in a way I have seen no other cat go. And so he would seek out any other cat or dog that might be there and straightway attack so impetuously that his antagonist never had a moment's time to collect itself for defence. This method seemed to be so demoralizing to both cats and dogs that I never saw a fight take place. The other fellow simply streaked off without asking any questions. Then William settled down beside me while I drank my beer until we both solemnly mounted our bicycle again and went on our way.

This was the cat who once, on the Lincolnshire Wolds,

brought in to me, for my edification and praise, a shrew with a white throat – the shrew that caused 'Barbellion' of the British Museum such joy when I took it to him. William just put it on my face as I slept in the tent under the fence. And then it had to be caught again all the way down inside my pyjamas. When William slept I do not know. He seemed to be busy all night catching and bringing in to me unconsidered trifles.

Once he caused us both to be mobbed and arrested by a crazy rabble of German spy hunters in the first week of the War. They had just looted a German pork butcher's shop, and then attacked me, for, as I heard one of them say: 'A man travelling with a cat on his shoulder must be a foreigner.' And, of course, a foreigner meant an enemy with such people in those gay days. We were escorted from the town by police in great state through a booing and sullen crowd until we had reached the quiet country once more and had a wash and brush up together.

The Legal Value of a Cat

Hoel Dha (Howell the Good), king of Wales in the tenth century, placed such a great value on cats, that he enacted the following laws.

The Vendotian Code Xl

The worth of a cat and her *teithi* (qualities) this is:

1st   The worth of a kitten from the night it is kittened until it shall open its eyes, is one penny.

2d   And from that time until it shall kill mice, two pence.

3d   And after it shall kill mice, four legal pence; and so it shall always remain.

4th   Her *teithe* are to see, to hear, to kill mice, and to have her claws.

The 'Dimentian Code'. XXXII

1st   The worth of a cat that is killed or stolen. Its head to be put downward upon a clean, even floor, with its tail lifted upward and thus suspended, whilst wheat is poured about it until the top of its tail be covered and that is to be its worth. If the corn cannot be had, then a milch sheep with a lamb and its wool is its value, if it be a cat that guards the king's barn.

2d   The worth of a common cat is four legal pence.

3d   The *teithi* of a cat, and of every animal upon the milk of which people do not feed, is the third part of its worth or the worth of its litter.

4th   Whosoever shall sell a cat (cath) is to answer that she devour not her kittens, and that she have ears, teeth, eyes, and nails, and be a good mouser.

The 'Gwentian Code'...

3d   That it be perfect of ear, perfect of eye, perfect of teeth, perfect of tail, perfect of claw, and without marks of fire. And if the cat fall short in any of these particulars, a third of her price had to be refunded. As to the fire, in case her fur had been singed the rats could detect her by the odour, and her qualities as a mouser were thus injured.

And then it goes on to say:

4th   That the *teithi* and the legal worth of a cat are coequal.

5th   A pound is the worth of a pet animal of the king.

6th   The pet animal of a breyer (brewer) is six score pence in value.

7th   The pet animal of a taoog is a curt penny in value.

Moppet

DOMINIQUE ENRIGHT

Moppet came to us with that name, not long after we arrived in Bangkok. Her owners, who were leaving the country, brought the young seal-point Siamese to us in an Alpine Sunbeam, a make of car that, on the few occasions I've seen one, still spells 'Siamese cat' to me. Stepping regally from her basket, the cat conducted a rapid tour of inspection, found all to her satisfaction, and settled down.

We recognized her beauty – silky cream with coffee, and the bluest eyes; we recognized her generally sociable nature – she won the hearts of many guests, while she was the only member of the family the naturalist Armand Denis found worthy of attention; and we recognized her intelligence – after one wet and unsuccessful attempt she had worked out that, if you want to drink from a vase (with flowers in it), you have to hold it with a paw in front as well as tip it forwards with a paw at the back.

She was still able to surprise us, though. One day, not many months after joining us, she stalked into the sitting room, giving muffled yowls of pride. Her jaws were firmly clamped just behind a snake's head. To make matters worse, we were pretty certain it was a poisonous snake. My parents caught hold of Moppet and prised open her jaws. This was a mistake as the snake immediately shot behind a very heavy teak multi-purpose article of furniture that had come with the house, and chaos ensued, as cat and I were bundled out, while my parents and the servants made a great deal of noise shouting and dragging the furniture round as they tried to catch the by now panicky and very angry snake. On the other side of the door, Moppet was clearly baffled by these strange human antics.

As for the snake, it vanished. A thorough search, with further thumps and banging, failed to unearth it, and we had to assume it had found a way out. We learned our lesson, and the next time Moppet caught a snake, we left her to it. She did not often catch them, but when she did, she never played with them, and never held them any place other than the back of the head so they could not turn to bite her. Having shown off her prowess, she would despatch the creature immediately with a quick bite and leave the otherwise undamaged corpse to be disposed of by a human.

Of course Moppet was wonderfully clean, fastidious in fact, and house-trained. So we were a bit surprised when a puddle appeared on the tiled bathroom floor. And a few days later very concerned when a small 'mess' appeared on the tiles. We had to suppose it was hers and asked her about it. She looked a bit sheepish, twitched her whiskers and found she needed urgently to have a quick wash. All was well afterwards . . . except there seemed to be someone who was not flushing the loo. Then one day I saw her, perched delicately on the loo seat. She had cottoned on to what to do. The sandbox was done away with, and we soon forgot that there was anything out of the ordinary in Moppet's accomplishment. Until early one morning an overnight guest woke my parents with excited cries. Having stumbled half-asleep into the spare bathroom, she had been jerked into wide-awakeness by the sight of a cat coolly observing her from the lavatory seat.

Moppet never did learn to use the flush, though.

Alas, poor Tiddles, we knew him well...

ANDREW PARSONS

(*The Times* Newspaper, 30th December 2000)

In the pantomime season, stages all over the country are crammed with grown men and women dressed up in black boots and fake whiskers. But while Pusses-in-Boots of the human variety are alive and well (and cracking some well-worn jokes), real theatre cats are a rare and precious breed, a remnant of the old, secret life of the stage.

Misty is the mottled, drizzle-grey cat who spends most of her off-duty hours curled up on a box of drapes under the stage at the Strand Theatre in London. Winches whirr and clink all around, and above her head the stage thunders with footsteps and voices. A new cast for the musical *Buddy* is in rehearsal. Misty is unperturbed. The only thing that bothers her is the two motorbikes which roar into life during the show. At which point she usually evaporates.

There was a time when every self-respecting theatre would have a Misty to slink around nonchalantly backstage and relieve the tension of waiting actors. Theatre cats were part of the creative, bohemian life of the stage, providing numerous unscripted moments when they wandered casually out in front of the audience, mid-scene.

Misty, at least, will reappear when the motorbike scenes are over, but in most theatres the working cats have gone, squeezed out by under-staffing, management efficiency and health and safety standards. And with them has gone some of the precious spark of unpredictability that characterised life in the theatre. Management has decided that rodent control may be less charismatic, but it does not fall asleep on the scenery, need a litter tray or make unprompted appearances stage left.

The Manchester Apollo still has Chess, a huge black-and-white cat that sleeps in the envelope box in the box office, but the Oxford Playhouse forcibly retired BC – Big Cat – four years ago, when its impromptu appearances on stage and its fur balls in dressing rooms became too much. BC's departure to a little old lady down the road so divided the crew that the stage manager and chief electrician did not speak to one another for a year.

The most celebrated of today's theatre cats are the pair at Shakespeare's Globe, a theatre which could not really afford to ignore the tradition. Jack and Cleo (stage names Portia and Brutus) took up their duties a couple of years ago, and since then even Turkish television has been in to film them. Nina Jacobs, the theatre's publicist, admits to finding the copious media coverage of the cats 'rather galling'.

'When we're trying to focus on the shows,' she says, 'cat publicity is not top of my priority list.'

The theatre is a superstitious place and for a long time cats were thought to bring luck to the house. Richard Huggett, in his book *The Curse of Macbeth*, even suggests that a cat's deposit in the dressing room is the luckiest of all omens, and reveals that this happened to Noël

Coward on the first night of *The Vortex*. The show went on to be a great success.

The actor Jon Holliday recalls a 1951 performance of *White Cargo*, at the Palace Theatre in Redditch, in which Felicity Kendal's father Geoffrey was co-star. 'The set was a hut in Africa, and the story was all about the white man's burden and how the heat and the demon drink destroy man's morals,' Holliday says.

'I was on stage with Geoffrey on the opening night, when on strolled the theatre tabby. Ignoring us, it walked leisurely to centre stage and peered over the footlights at the audience. 'Get that tiger out of here,' commanded Geoffrey.'

Some cats have survived in the West End, but they lead a rather less glamorous existence, confined almost exclusively to front of house. Marilyn (after Monroe) and Vivien (Leigh), for example, are habitually to be found stretched out on top of box-office computers in the Comedy Theatre on Panton Street. 'Marilyn spends so much of her time asleep that we sometimes worry that she's passed on,' says Simon Francis, the theatre manager.

The Albery, situated in a nest of restaurant-lined alleys in St Martin's Lane, is Top Cat territory. Its two pets are called Girl Cat and Boy Cat ('because of what they used to do to each other') and, as their names suggest, they are a savvy pair, acquired originally because of a burgeoning mouse problem.

Although still in the early stages of his career, Boy Cat has already eaten Princess Margaret's bouquet at a gala evening. During a performance of *Pygmalion* he walked across the stage, jumped down into the audience and sat in a vacant seat in the front row, where one of the audience stroked him for the rest of the show.

In *Five Guys Named Moe* both cats got stuck under a box on stage and refused to come out until the tap-dancing began over their heads, whereupon they made a circuit of the auditorium, chased by ushers.

Today's cats are rarely allowed anywhere near the cast, but that has not always been the case. Beryl Reid, a cat enthusiast who took the Lyric's pet, Fleur, home with her, maintained that theatre cats were an effective antidote to stage-fright.

'The act of stroking a cat is a great reliever of tension and brings down the blood pressure,' she wrote.

One of Reid's favourites was Beerbohm, former resident of what is now The Gielgud. An aristocratic tabby, whose portrait still hangs in the corridor towards the stalls, Beerbohm used to put in an appearance on stage at least once in every production, testing the actors' ability to improvise. Although he was friendly to most cast members, his general policy was to select one – Peter Bowles, Michael Gambon or Penelope Keith, for example – for special treatment and occupy their dressing room for the duration. Beerbohm's celebrity earned him several mentions on *Desert Island Discs*, and he is the only theatre cat to have been honoured with a front-page obituary in *The Stage* newspaper.

In 1974,The Theatre Royal, Drury Lane, was enjoying some success with *Billy*, starring Michael Crawford, so, when it acquired a new cat, the stagehands called it Ambrose after a scene in the show. Ambrose was dressed permanently in evening wear – jet black coat with a white chest – and was generally loved by all. But he did enjoy his live appearances, which more than aggravated the leading man. The audience would laugh and sometimes applaud. 'It was difficult to keep a straight face,' recalls Marianne Price, who was playing opposite Crawford at the time, but the actor himself was incensed. 'He hated being upstaged,' says Price. All sorts of dark threats were made, but the backstage crew lined up in solid defence of Ambrose.

The actress Avis Bunnage was part of the production and she, too, fell in love with Ambrose.

It was all she could do to tear herself away from the

theatre when *Billy* came to an end. After leaving, Bunnage began a remarkable 12-year correspondence with both Ambrose and Thora Tolson, the theatre secretary, which reveals a fierce jealousy for Ambrose's affections.

In May 1976 Bunnage wrote to Tolson: 'I think about Ambrose constantly, and miss him very much. If he does show any signs of pining, I'm sure you will let me know, and trust that 'they' will let me take him. I know John feeds him ... but a lot of men don't understand ...'

In 1983 both Bunnage and Ambrose were unwell. In August, Bunnage wrote again to Tolson with a cheque. 'Please accept the enclosed towards Ambrose's expenses. Whatever it costs to make him well, I will pay.' Ambrose died in 1985 and Bunnage was heartbroken. The Theatre Royal, Drury Lane, has not had a cat since.

Strange Friends

MARK TWAIN

In *The Innocents Abroad*, the American author and cat lover wrote of an unlikely alliance he discovered while travelling in France in 1869.

In the great Zoological Gardens [of Marseilles], we found specimens of all the animals the world produces, I think.... The boon companion of the colossal elephant was a common cat! This cat had a fashion of climbing up the elephant's hind legs, and roosting on his back. She would sit up there, with her paws curved under her breast, and sleep in the sun half the afternoon. It used to annoy the elephant at first and he would reach up and take her down, but she would go aft and climb up again. She persisted until she finally conquered the elephant's prejudices, and now they are inseparable friends. The cat plays about her comrade's forefeet or his trunk often, until dogs approach, and then she goes aloft out of danger. The elephant has annihilated several dogs lately, that pressed his companion too closely.

Nelson, the Brave

Winston Churchill, the great wartime leader, had a pet cat called Nelson, who, during air raids, would make his way to his own shelter (probably driven by the noise of the anti-aircraft fire rather than the prospect of being bombed): under a heavy chest of drawers in the Prime Minister's bedroom. His master, on the other hand, would not be budged from wherever he happened to be when these airborne attacks commenced.

Churchill's Private Secretary, Jock Colville, recounts in his memoirs, *Footprints in Time*, that one afternoon there was an air raid, and he made his way to the Prime Minister's bedroom, ostensibly to deliver a telegram from Roosevelt, but in reality to try to persuade his boss to repair to the air-raid shelter – a vain task no one enjoyed as they knew they would receive short shrift from Churchill.

Colville knocked on the door, but there was no reply, so he went in to find a scantily-clad Churchill on all fours, peering under the massive chest of drawers.

'You should be ashamed of yourself,' he was saying into the dark shadows beneath it, 'with a name like yours, skulking under this chest of drawers while all those brave young men in the RAF are up there fighting gallantly to save their country.'

But Nelson stayed where he was until the din – and the recriminations – died away.

My Boss the Cat

PAUL GALLICO

If you are thinking of acquiring a cat at your house and would care for a quick sketch of what your life will be like under *Felis domesticus*, you have come to the right party. I have figured out that, to date, I have worked for – and I mean *worked* for – thirty-nine of these four-legged characters, including one memorable period when I was doing the bidding of some twenty-three assorted resident felines all at the same time.

Cats are, of course, no good. They're chisellers and panhandlers, sharpers and shameless flatterers. They're as full of schemes and plans, plots and counterplots, wiles and guiles as any confidence man. They can read your character better than a $50-an-hour psychiatrist. They know to a milligram how much of the old oil to pour on to break you down. They are definitely smarter than I am, which is one reason why I love 'em.

Cat-haters will try to floor you with the old argument, 'If cats are so smart, why can't they do tricks, the way dogs do?' It isn't that cats can't do tricks; it's that they *won't*. They're far too hep to stand up and beg for food when they know in advance you'll give it to them anyway. And as for rolling over, or playing dead, or 'speaking', what's in it for pussy that isn't already hers?

Cats, incidentally, are a great warm-up for a successful

93

marriage – they teach you your place in the household. The first thing Kitty does is to organize your home on a comfortable basis – *her* basis. She'll eat when she wants to; she'll go out at her pleasure. She'll come in when she gets good and ready, if at all.

She wants attention when she wants it and darned well means to be let alone when she has other things on her mind. She is jealous; she won't have you showering attentions or caresses on any other minxes, whether two or four-footed.

She gets upset when you come home late and when you go away on a business trip. But when *she* decides to stay out a couple of nights, it is none of your darned business where she's been or what she's been up to. Either you trust her or you don't.

She hates dirt, bad smells, poor food, loud noises and people you bring home unexpectedly to dinner.

Kitty also has her share of small-child obstinacy. She enjoys seeing you flustered, fussed, red in the face and losing your temper. Sometimes, as she hangs about watching, you get the feeling that it is all she can do to keep from busting out laughing. And she's got the darndest knack for putting the entire responsibility for everything on *you*.

For instance, Kitty pretends that she can neither talk nor understand you, and that she is therefore nothing but a poor helpless dumb animal. What a laugh! Any self-respecting racket-working cat can make you understand at all times exactly what she wants. She has one voice for 'Let's eat,' another for wanting out, still a third for 'You don't happen to have seen my toy mouse around here, the one with the tail chewed off?' and a host of other easily identifiable speeches. She can also understand you perfectly, if she thinks there's profit in it.

I once had a cat I suspected of being able to read. This was a gent named Morris, a big tabby with topaz eyes who lived with me when I was batching it in a New York apartment. One day I had just finished writing to a lady who at that time was the object of my devotion. Naturally I brought considerable of the writer's art into telling her this. I was called to the telephone for a few minutes. When I returned, Morris was sitting on my desk reading the letter. At least, he was staring down at it, looking a little ill. He gave me that long, baffled look of which cats are capable, and immediately meowed to be let out. He didn't come back for three days. Thereafter I kept my private correspondence locked up.

The incident reminds me of another highly discriminating cat I had down on the farm by the name of Tante Hedwig. One Sunday a guest asked me whether I could make a cocktail called a Mexican. I said I thought I could, and proceeded to blend a horror of gin, pineapple juice, vermouth, bitters, and other ill- assorted ingredients. Pouring out a trial glass, I spilled it on the grass. Tante Hedwig came over, sniffed and, with a look of shameful embarrassment, solicitously covered it over. Everybody agreed later that she had something there.

Let me warn you not to put too much stock in the theory that animals do not think and that they act only by instinct. Did you ever try to keep a cat out that wanted to come in, or vice versa? I once locked a cat in the cellar. He climbed a straight, smooth cement wall, hung on with his paws (I saw the claw marks to prove it); unfastened the window-hook with his nose and climbed out.

Cats have fabulous memories, I maintain, and also the ability to measure and evaluate what they remember. Take, for instance, our two Ukrainian greys, Chin and Chilla. My wife brought them up on a medicine dropper. We gave them love and care and a good home on a farm in New Jersey.

Eventually we had to travel abroad, so Chin and Chilla went to live with friends in Glenview, Ill., a pretty snazzy place. Back in the United States, we went out to spend Thanksgiving in Glenview. We looked forward, among other things, to seeing our two cats. When we arrived at the house, Chin and Chilla were squatting at the top of a broad flight of stairs. As we called up a tender greeting to them, we saw an expression of horror come over their faces. 'Great heavens! It's those *paupers*! Run!' With that, they vanished and could not be found for five hours. They were frightened to death we had come to take them back to the squalor of a country estate in New Jersey, and deprive them of a room of their own in Illinois, with glassed-in sun porch, screens for their toilets and similar super-luxuries.

After a time they made a grudging appearance and consented to play the old games and talk over old times, guardedly. But when the hour arrived for our departure, they vanished once more. Our hostess wrote us that apparently they got hold of a timetable somewhere and waited until our train was past Elkhart before coming out.

It was this same Chilla who, one day on the farm after our big ginger cat, Wuzzy, had been missing for forty-eight hours, led us to where he was, a half mile away, out of sight and out of hearing, caught in a trap. Every so often Chilla would look back to see if we were coming. Old Wuz was half-dead when we got there, but when he saw Chilla he started to purr.

Two-Timing, or Leading the Double Life, is something you may be called upon to face with your cat. It means simply that Kitty manages to divide her time between two homes sufficiently far apart that each home-owner thinks she is his.

I discovered this when trying to check up on the unaccountable absences of Lulu II, a seal-point Siamese. I finally located her at the other end of the bay, mooching on an amiable spinster. When I said, 'Oh, I hope that my Lulu hasn't been imposing on you,' she replied indignantly, '*Your* Lulu! You mean *our* dear little Pitipoo! We've been wondering where she went when she disappeared occasionally. We do hope she hasn't been annoying *you*.'

The shocking part of this story, of course, is that, for the sake of a hand-out, Lulu, with a pedigree as long as your arm, was willing to submit to being called Pitipoo.

Of all things a smart cat does to whip you into line, the gift of the captured mouse is the cleverest and most touching. There was Limpy, the wild barn cat down on the farm who lived off what she caught in the fields. We were already supporting four cats, but in the winter, when we went to town, we brought her along.

We had not been inside the apartment ten minutes before Limpy caught a mouse, or probably *the* mouse, and at once brought it over and laid it at our feet. Now, as indicated before, Limpy had hunted to survive. To Limpy a dead mouse was Big and Little Casino, a touch-down home run and Grand Slam. Yet this one she gave to us.

How can you mark it up except as rent, or thanks, or 'Here, looka; this is the most important thing I do. You take it because I like you'? You can teach a dog to retrieve and bring you game, but only a cat will voluntarily hand over its kill to you as an unsolicited gift.

How come Kitty acts not like the beast of prey she is but like a better-class human being? I don't know the answer. The point is, she does it – and makes you her slave ever after. Once you have been presented with a mouse by your cat, you will never be the same again. She can use you for a door-mat. And she will, too.

From

The Cat by the Fire

LEIGH HUNT

A blazing fire, a warm rug, candles lit and curtains drawn, the kettle on for tea (nor do the 'first circles' despise the preference of a kettle to an urn, as the third or fourth may do), and, finally, the cat before you, attracting your attention – it is a scene which everybody likes unless he has a morbid aversion to cats; which is not common. There are some nice inquirers, it is true, who are apt to make uneasy comparisons of cats with dogs – to say they are not so loving, that they prefer the house to the man, et cetera. But agreeably to the good old maxim, that 'comparisons are odious,' our readers, we hope, will continue to like what is likable in anything, for its own sake, without trying to render it unlikable from its inferiority to something else – a process by which we might ingeniously contrive to put soot into every dish that is set before us, and to reject one thing after another, till we were pleased with nothing. Here is a good fireside, and a cat to it; and it would be our own fault, if, in removing to another house and another fireside, we did not take care that the cat removed with us. Cats cannot look to the moving of goods, as men do. If we would have creatures considerate toward us, we must be so toward them. It is not to be expected of everybody, quadruped or biped, that they should stick to us in spite of our want of merit, like a dog or a benevolent sage. Besides, stories have been told of cats very much to the credit of their benignity; such as their following a master about like a dog, waiting at a gentleman's door to thank him for some obligation overnight, et cetera. And our readers may remember the history of the famous Godolphin Arabian, upon whose grave a cat that had lived with him in the stable went and stretched itself, and died.

The cat purrs, as if it applauded our consideration – and gently moves its tail. What an odd expression of the power to be irritable and the will to be pleased there is in its face, as it looks up at us! We must own that we do not prefer a cat in the act of purring, or of looking in that manner. It reminds us of the sort of smile, or simmer (*simper* is too weak and fleeting a word) that is apt to be in the faces of irritable people when they are pleased to be in a state of satisfaction. We prefer, for a general expression, the cat in a quiet, unpretending state, and the human countenance with a look indicative of habitual grace and composure, as if it were not necessary to take any violent steps to prove its amiability – the 'smile without a smile,' as the poet beautifully calls it.

Furthermore (in order to get rid at once of all that may be objected to poor Pussy, as boys at school get down their bad dumpling as fast as possible before the meat comes), we own we have an objection to the way in which a cat sports with a mouse before she kills it, tossing and jerking it about like a ball, and letting it go, in order to pounce upon it with the greater relish. And yet what right have we to apply human measures of cruelty to the inferior reflectability of a cat? Perhaps she has no idea of the mouse's being alive, in the sense that we have – most likely she looks upon it as a pleasant movable toy, made to be eaten – a sort of lively pudding, that oddly jumps hither and thither. It would be hard to beat into the head of a country squire of the old class that there is any cruelty in hunting a hare; and most assuredly it would be still harder to beat mouse-sparing into the head of a cat. You might read the most pungent essay on the subject into her ear, and she would only sneeze at it.

As to the unnatural cruelties which we sometimes read of, committed by cats upon their offspring, they are exceptions to the common and beautiful rules of nature, and accordingly we have nothing to do with them. They are traceable to some unnatural circumstances of breeding or position. Enormities as monstrous are to be found among human beings, and argue nothing against the general character of the species. Even dogs are not always immaculate; and sages have made slips. Dr Franklin cut off his son with a shilling for differing with him in politics.

But cats resemble tigers? They are tigers in miniature? Well – and very pretty miniatures they are. And what has the tiger himself done, that he has not a right to eat his dinner as well as Jones? A tiger treats a man much as a cat does a mouse – granted; but we have no reason to suppose that he is aware of the man's sufferings, or means anything but to satisfy his hunger; and what have the butcher and poulterer been about meanwhile? The tiger, it is true, lays about him a little superfluously sometimes, when he gets into a sheepfold, and kills more than he eats; but does not the squire or the marquis do pretty much like him in the month of September? Nay, do we not hear of venerable judges that would not hurt a fly going about in that refreshing month, seeking whom they may lame? See the effect of habit and education! And you can educate the tiger in no other way than by attending to his stomach. Fill that, and he will want no men to eat, probably not even to lame. On the other hand, deprive Jones of his dinner for a day or two, and see what a state he will be in, especially if he is by nature irascible. Nay, keep him from it for a half an hour, and observe the tiger propensities of his stomach and fingers – how worthy of killing he thinks the cook, and what boxes of the ear he feels inclined to give the footboy.

Animals, by the nature of things, in their present state dispose of one another into their respective stomachs, without ill will on any side. They keep down the several populations of their neighbours, till time may come when superfluous population of any kind need not exist, and predatory appearances may vanish from the earth, as the wolves have done from England. But whether they may or not is not a question by a hundred times so important to moral inquirers as into the possibilities of human education and the nonsense of ill will. Show the nonentity of that, and we may all get our dinners as jovially as we can, sure of these three undoubted facts – that life is long, death short, and the world beautiful. And so we bring our thoughts back again to the fireside, and look at the cat.

Poor Pussy! She looks up at us again, as if she thanked us for those vindications of dinner; and symbolically gives a twist of a yawn and a lick to her whiskers. Now she proceeds to clean herself all over, having a just sense of the demands of her elegant person, beginning judiciously with her paws, and fetching amazing tongues at her hind hips. Anon, she scratches her neck with a foot of rapid delight, leaning her head toward it, and shutting her eyes, half to accommodate the action of the skin, and half to enjoy the luxury. She then rewards her paws with a few more touches – look at the action of her head and neck, how pleasing it is, the ears pointed forward, and the neck gently arching to and fro. Finally, she gives a sneeze and another twist of mouth and whiskers, and then, curling her tail toward her front claws, settles herself on her hindquarters, in an attitude of bland meditation.

What does she think of? Of her saucer of milk at breakfast? Or of the thump she got yesterday in the kitchen for stealing the meat? Or of her own meat, the Tartar's dish, noble horseflesh? Or of her friend the cat next door, the most impassioned of serenaders? Or of her little ones, some of whom are now large, and all of them gone? Is *that* among her recollections when she looks pensive? Does she taste of the noble prerogative sorrows of man?

She is a sprightly cat, hardly past her youth; so, happening to move the fringe of the rug a little with our foot, she darts out a paw, and begins plucking it and inquiring into the matter, as if it were a challenge to play, or something lively enough to be eaten. What a graceful action of that foot of hers, between delicacy and petulance – combining something of a thrust out, a beat, and a scratch. There seems even something of a little bit of fear in it, as if just enough to provoke her courage, and give her the excitement of a sense of hazard. We remember being much amused with seeing a kitten manifestly making a series of experiments upon the patience of its mother – trying how far the latter would put up with positive bites and thumps. The kitten ran at her every moment, gave her a knock or a bite of the tail; and then ran back again, to recommence the assault. The mother sat looking at her, as if betwixt tolerance and admiration, to see how far the spirit of the family was inherited or improved by her sprightly offspring. At length, however, the 'little Pickle' presumed too far, and the mother, lifting up her paw, and meeting her at the very nick of the moment, gave her one of the most unsophisticated boxes of the ear we ever beheld. It sent her rolling half over the room, and made her come to a most ludicrous pause, with the oddest little look of premature and wincing meditation.

The lapping of the milk out of the saucer is what one's human thirst cannot sympathize with. It seems as if there could be no satisfaction in such a series of atoms of drink. Yet the saucer is soon emptied; and there is a refreshment to one's ears in that sound of plashing with which the action is accompanied and which seems indicative of a like comfort to Pussy's mouth. Her tongue is thin and can make a spoon of itself. This, however, is common to other quadrupeds with the cat, and does not, therefore, more particularly belong to our feline consideration. Not so the electricity of its coat, which gives out sparks under the hand; its passion for the herb valerian (Did the reader ever see one roll in it? It is a mad sight) and other singular delicacies of nature, among which, perhaps, is to be reckoned its taste for fish, a creature with whose element it has so little to do that it is supposed even to abhor it; though lately we read somewhere of a swimming cat that used to fish for itself. And this reminds us of an exquisite anecdote of dear, dogmatic, diseased, thoughtful, surly, charitable Johnson, who would go out of doors himself and buy oysters for his cat, because his black servant was too proud to do it! Not that we condemn the black, in those enslaving, unliberating days. He had a right to the mistake, though we should have thought better of him had he seen further, and subjected his pride to affection for such a master. But Johnson's true practical delicacy in the matter is beautiful. Be assured that he thought nothing of 'condescension' in it, or of being eccentric. He was singular in some things, because he could not help it. But he hated eccentricity. No, in his best moments he felt himself simply to be a man, and a good man too, though a frail – one that in virtue as well as humility, and in a knowledge of his ignorance as well as his wisdom, was desirous of being a Christian philosopher; and accordingly he went out, and bought food for his hungry cat, because his poor Negro was too proud to do it, and there was nobody else in the way whom he had a right to ask. What must anybody that saw him have thought as he turned up Bolt Court! But doubtless he went as secretly as possible — that is to say, if he considered the thing at all. His friend Garrick could not have done as much! He was too grand, and on the great stage of life. Goldsmith could, but he would hardly have thought of it. Beauclerc might, but he would have thought it necessary to excuse it with a jest or a wager, or some such thing. Sir Joshua Reynolds, with his fashionable, fine-lady-painting hand, would certainly have shrunk from it. Burke would have reasoned himself into its propriety, but he would have reasoned himself out again. Gibbon! Imagine its being put into the head of Gibbon!! He and his bagwig would have started with all the horror of a gentleman usher; and he would have rung the bell for the cook's-deputy's-under-assistant-errand-boy.

Cats at firesides live luxuriously and are the picture of comfort; but lest they should not bear their portion of trouble in this world, they have the drawbacks of being liable to be shut out of doors on cold nights, beatings from the 'aggravated' cooks, overpettings of children (how should we like to be squeezed and pulled about in that manner by some great patronizing giants?), and last, not least, horrible merciless tramples of unconscious human feet and unfeeling legs of chairs. Elegance, comfort, and security seem the order of the day on all sides, and you are going to sit down to dinner, or to music, or to take tea, when all of a sudden the cat gives a squall as if she were mashed; and you are not sure that the fact is otherwise. Yet she gets in the way again, as before, and dares all the feet and mahogany in the room. Beautiful present sufficingness of a cat's imagination! Confined to the snug circle of her own sides, and the two next inches of rug or carpet.

Waiting for the Bar to Open

CARL VAN VECHTEN

This delightful excerpt is taken from Van Vechten's famous book, *The Tiger in the House*, published in 1922.

O ne very hot August Sunday afternoon walking up Fifth Avenue, I observed a large orange tabby tom rubbing himself against a hydrant and mewing. I stopped to speak with him, as is my custom with cats, when an Irish policeman approached.

'I believe he wants a drink,' suggested this very intelligent officer. 'He's noticed that water sometimes comes from that hydrant.'

'I think you are right,' I replied. 'Let's get him one.'

Now a cat will not take an excursion merely because a man wants a walking companion. Walking is a human habit into which dogs readily fall but it is a distasteful form of exercise to a cat unless he has a purpose in view. I have never known a cat with a purpose in view to refuse a walk. This case was no exception. The orange tabby was a complete stranger to both the policeman and myself and yet when we suggested a little drink he walked peaceably a little way behind us as we strolled down Fifth Avenue.

'I think Page and Shaw's is open,' said the policeman.

Now Page and Shaw's was three blocks below the hydrant and yet that cat followed at our heels. When we arrived at the shop I asked Tom to sit down for a moment; the policeman went in and presently emerged with a paper cup full of water. Tom drank every bit of this and then asked for more. He had another cup. Then, having no further use for us, without a word or gesture he trotted off.

The Fat Cat

Q. PATRICK

The marines found her when they finally captured the old mission house at Fufa. After two days of relentless pounding, they hadn't expected to find anything alive there -least of all a fat cat.

And she was a very fat cat, sandy as a Scotsman, with enormous agate eyes and a fat amiable face. She sat there on the mat-or rather what was left of the mat-in front of what had been the mission porch, licking her paws as placidly as if the shell-blasted jungle were a summer lawn in New Jersey.

One of the men, remembering his childhood primer, quoted: 'The fat cat sat on the mat.'

The other men laughed; not that the remark was really funny, but laughter broke the tension and expressed their relief at having at last reached their objective, after two days of bitter fighting.

The fat cat, still sitting on the mat, smiled at them, as if to show she didn't mind the joke being on her. Then she saw Corporal Randy Jones, and for some reason known only to herself ran toward him as though he was her long-lost master. With a refrigerator purr, she weaved in and out of his muddy legs.

Everyone laughed again as Randy picked her up and pushed his ugly face against the sleek fur. It was funny to see any living thing show a preference for the dour, solitary Randy.

A sergeant flicked his fingers. 'Kitty. Come here. We'll make you B Company mascot.'

But the cat, perched on Randy's shoulder like a queen on her throne, merely smiled down majestically as much as to say: 'You can be my subjects if you like. But this is my man-my royal consort.'

And never for a second did she swerve from her devotion. She lived with Randy, slept with him, ate only food provided by him. Almost every man in Co. B tried to seduce her with caresses and morsels of canned ration, but all advances were met with a yawn of contempt.

For Randy this new love was ecstasy. He guarded her with the possessive tenderness of a mother. He combed her fur sleek; he almost starved himself to maintain her fatness. And all the time there was a strange wonder in him. The homeliest and ungainliest of ten in a West Virginia mining family, he had never before aroused affection in man or woman. No one had counted for him until the fat cat.

Randy's felicity, however, was short-lived. In a few days B Company was selected to carry out a flanking movement to surprise and possibly capture the enemy's headquarters, known to be twenty miles away through dense, sniper-infested jungle. The going would be rugged. Each man would carry his own supply of food and water, and sleep in foxholes with no support from the base.

The C.O. was definite about the fat cat: the stricken Randy was informed that the presence of a cat would seriously endanger the safety of the whole company. If it were seen following him, it would be shot on sight. just before their scheduled departure, Randy carried the fat cat over to the mess of Co. H, where she was enthusiastically received by an equally fat cook. Randy could not bring himself to look back at the reproachful stare which he knew would be in the cat's agate eyes.

But all through that first day of perilous jungle travel, the thought of the cat's stare haunted him, and he was prey to all the heartache of parting; in leaving the cat, he had left behind wife, mother, and child.

Darkness, like an immense black parachute, had descended hours ago on the jungle, when Randy was awakened from exhausted sleep. Something soft and warm was brushing his cheek; and his foxhole resounded to a symphony of purring. He stretched out an incredulous hand, but this was no dream. Real and solid, the cat was curled in a contented ball at his shoulder.

His first rush of pleasure was chilled as he remembered his C.O.'s words. The cat, spurning the blandishments of H. Co.'s cuisine, had followed him through miles of treacherous jungle, only to face death the moment daylight revealed her presence.

Randy was in an agony of uncertainty. To carry her back to the base would be desertion. To beat and drive her away was beyond the power of his simple nature.

The cat nuzzled his face again and breathed a mournful meow. She was hungry, of course, after her desperate trek. Suddenly Randy saw what he must do. If he could bring himself not to feed her, hunger would surely drive her back to the sanctuary of the cook.

She meowed again. He shushed her and gave her a half hearted slap. "Aain't got nothing for you, honey. Scram. Go home. Scat.'

To his mingled pleasure and disappointment, she leaped silently out of the foxhole. When morning came there was no sign of her.

As B Company inched its furtive advance through the dense undergrowth, Randy felt the visit from the cat must have been a dream. But on the third night it came again. It brushed against his cheek and daintily took his ear in its teeth. When it meowed, the sound was still soft and cautious, but held a pitiful quaver of beseechment which cut through Randy like a Jap bayonet.

On its first visit, Randy had not seen the cat, but tonight some impulse made him reach for his flashlight. Holding it carefully downward, he turned it on. What he saw was the ultimate ordeal. The fat cat was fat no longer. Her body sagged; her sleek fur was matted and mud-stained, her paws torn and bloody. But it was the eyes, blinking up at him, that were the worst. There was no hint of reproach in them, only an expression of infinite trust and pleading.

Forgetting everything but those eyes, Randy tugged out one of his few remaining cans of ration. At the sight of it, the cat weakly licked its lips. Randy moved to open the can. Then the realization that he would be signing the cat's death warrant surged over him. And, because the pent-up emotion in him had to have some outlet, it turned into unreasoning anger against this animal whose suffering had become more than he could bear. 'Skat,' he hissed. But the cat did not move.

He lashed out at her with the heavy flashlight. For a second she lay motionless under the blow. Then with a little moan she fled.

The next night she did not come back and Randy did not sleep.

On the fifth day they reached really dangerous territory. Randy and another marine, Joe, were sent forward to scout for the Jap command headquarters. Suddenly, weaving through the jungle, they came upon it.

A profound silence hung over the glade, with its two hastily erected shacks. Peering through the dense foliage, they saw traces of recent evacuation -waste paper scattered on the grass, a pile of fresh garbage, a Jap army shirt flapping on a tree. Outside one of the shacks, under an awning, stretched a rough table strewn with the remains of a meal. 'They must have got wind of us and scrammed,' breathed Joe.

Randy edged forward-then froze as something stirred in the long grasses near the door of the first shack. As he watched, the once fat cat hobbled out into the sunlight.

A sense of heightened danger warred with Randy's pride that she had not abandoned him. Stiff with suspense, he watched it disappear into the shack. Soon it padded out.

'No Japs,' said Joe. 'That cat'd have raised 'em sure as shooting.'

He started boldly into the glade. 'Hey, Randy, there's a whole chicken on that table. Chicken's going to taste good after K ration.'

He broke off, for the cat had seen the chicken too, and with pitiful clumsiness had leaped on to the table. With an angry yell Joe stooped for a rock and threw it.

Indignation blazed in Randy. He'd starved and spurned the cat, and yet she'd followed him with blind devotion. The chicken, surely, should be her reward. In his slow, simple mind it seemed the most important thing in the world for his beloved to have her fair share of the booty.

The cat, seeing the rock coming, lumbered off the table just in time, for the rock struck the chicken squarely, knocking it off its plate.

Randy leaped into the clearing. As he did so, a deafening explosion made him drop to the ground. A few seconds later, when he raised himself, there was no table, no shack, nothing but a blazing wreckage of wood.

Dazedly he heard Joe's voice: 'Booby trap under that chicken. Gee, if that cat hadn't jumped for it, I wouldn't have hurled the rock; we'd have grabbed it ourselves-and we'd be in heaven now.' His voice dropped to an awed whisper. 'That cat. I guess it's blown to hell ... But it saved our lives.' Randy couldn't speak. There was a constriction in his throat. He lay there, feeling more desolate than hed ever felt in his life before.

Then from behind came a contented purr. He spun round. Freakishly, the explosion had hurled a crude rush mat out of the shack. It had come to rest on the grass behind him. And, seated serenely on the mat, the cat was smiling at him.

From
Jubilate Agno

CHRISTOPHER SMART

When poet Christopher Smart (1722-71) was confined in a London madhouse for seven years, his only companion was Jeoffry, his cat. Smart wrote about Jeoffry in a long poem called '*Jubilate Agno*' (Rejoice in the Lamb'), part of which is reproduced here.

For I will consider my Cat Jeoffry.
For he is the servant of the Living God duly and daily serving him.
For at the first glance of the glory of God in the East he worships in his way.
For this is done by wreathing his body seven times round with elegant quickness.
For then he leaps up to catch the musk, which is the blessing of God upon his prayer.
For he rolls upon prank to work it in.
For having done duty and received blessing he begins to consider himself.
For this he performs in ten degrees.
For first he looks upon his forepaws to see if they are clean.
For secondly he kicks up behind to clear away there.
For thirdly he works it upon stretch with the forepaws extended.

For fourthly he sharpens his paws by wood.

For fifthly he washes himself.

For sixthly he rolls upon wash.

For seventhly he fleas himself, that he may not be interrupted upon the beat.

For eighthly he rubs himself against a post.

For ninthly he looks up for his instructions.

For tenthly he goes in quest of food.

For having consider'd God and himself he will consider his neighbour.

For if he meets another cat he will kiss her in kindness.

For when he takes his prey he plays with it to give it a chance.

For one mouse in seven escapes by his dallying.

For when his day's work is done his business more properly begins.

For he keeps the Lord's watch in the night against the adversary.

For he counteracts the powers of darkness by his electrical skin and glaring eyes.

For he counteracts the Devil, who is death, by brisking about the life.

For in his morning orisons he loves the sun and the sun loves him.

For he is of the tribe of Tiger.

For the Cherub Cat is a term of the Angel Tiger.

For he has the subtlety and hissing of a serpent, which in goodness he suppresses.

For he will not do destruction, if he is well-fed, neither will he spit without provocation.

For he purrs in thankfulness, when God tells him he's a good Cat.

For he is an instrument for the children to learn benevolence upon.

For every house is incomplete without him and a blessing is lacking in the spirit.

For the Lord commanded Moses concerning the cats at

the departure of the Children of Israel from Egypt.

For every family had one cat at least in the bag.

For the English Cats are the best in Europe.

For he is the cleanest in the use of his forepaws of any quadrupede.

For the dexterity of his defence is an instance of the love of God to him exceedingly.

For he is the quickest to his mark of any creature.

For he is tenacious of his point.

For he is a mixture of gravity and waggery.

For he knows that God is his Saviour.

For there is nothing sweeter than his peace when at rest.

For there is nothing brisker than his life when in motion.

For he is of the Lord's poor and so indeed is he called by benevolence perpetually – Poor Jeoffry! poor Jeoffry! the rat has bit thy throat.

For I bless the name of the Lord Jesus that Jeoffry is better.

For the divine spirit comes about his body to sustain it in complete cat.

For his tongue is exceeding pure so that it has in purity what it wants in music.

For he is docile and can learn certain things.

For he can set up with gravity which is patience upon approbation.

For he can fetch and carry, which is patience in employment.

For he can jump over a stick which is patience upon proof positive.

For he can spraggle upon waggle at the word of command.

For he can jump from an eminence into his master's bosom.

For he can catch the cork and toss it again.

For he is hated by the hypocrite and miser.

For the former is afraid of detection.

For the latter refuses the charge.

For he camels his back to bear the first notion of business.

For he is good to think on, if a man would express himself neatly.

For he made a great figure in Egypt for his signal services.

For he killed the Ichneumon-rat very pernicious by land.

For his ears are so acute that they sting again.

For from this proceeds the passing quickness of his attention.

For by stroking of him I have found out electricity.

For I perceived God's light about him both wax and fire.

For the Electrical fire is the spiritual substance, which God sends from heaven to sustain the bodies both of man and beast.

For God has blessed him in the variety of his movements.

For, tho he cannot fly, he is an excellent clamberer.

For his motions upon the face of the earth are more than any other quadrupede.

For he can tread to all the measures upon the music.

For he can swim for life.

For he can creep.

Rufus the Survivor

DORIS LESSING

Events did cast their shadow, months before. All that spring and summer, as I went past on the pavement, a shabby orange-coloured cat would emerge from under a car or from a front garden, and he stood looking intently up at me, not to be ignored. He wanted something, but what? Cats on pavements, cats on garden walls, or coming towards you from doorways, stretch and wave their tails, they greet you, walk a few steps with you. They want companionship or, if they are shut out by heartless owners, as they often are all day or all night, they appeal for help with the loud insistent demanding miaow that means they are hungry or thirsty or cold. A cat winding around your legs at a street corner might be wondering if he can exchange a poor home for a better one. But this cat did not miaow, he only looked, a thoughtful, hard stare from yellow-grey eyes. Then he began following me along the pavement in a tentative way, looking up at me. He presented himself to me when I came in and when I went out, and he was on my conscience. Was he hungry? I took some food out to him and put it under a car, and he ate a little, but left the rest. Yet he was necessitous, desperate, I knew that. Did he have a home in our street, and was it a bad one? He

118

seemed most often to be near a house some doors down from ours and, once, when an old woman went in, he went in too. So he was not homeless. Yet he took to following me to our gate and once, when the pavement filled with a surge of shouting schoolchildren, he scrambled into our little front garden, terrified, and watched me at the door.

He was thirsty, not hungry. Or so thirsty, hunger was the lesser demand. That was the summer of 1984, with long stretches of warm weather. Cats locked out of their homes all day without water suffered. I put down a basin of water on my front porch one night and in the morning it was empty. Then, as the hot weather went on, I put another basin on my back balcony, reached by way of a lilac tree and a big jump up from a small roof. And this basin, too, was empty every morning. One hot dusty day there was the orange cat on the back balcony crouched over the water basin, drinking, drinking ... He finished all the water and wanted more. I refilled the basin and again he crouched down and emptied that. This meant there must be something wrong with his kidneys. Now I could take my time looking at him. A scruffy cat, his dirty fur rough over knobbly bones. But he was a wonderful colour, fire colour, like a fox. He was, as they put it, a whole cat, he had his two neat furry balls under his tail. His ears were torn, scarred with fighting. Now, when I came in and out of the house, he was no longer there in the street, he had moved from the fronts of the houses and the precarious life there with the speeding cars and the shouting, running children, to the back scene of long untidy gardens and shrubs and trees, and many birds and cats. He was on our little balcony where there are plants in pots, bounded by a low wall. Over this the lilac tree holds out its boughs, always full of birds. He lay in the strip of shade under the wall, and the water bowl was always empty, and when he saw me he stood up and waited beside it for more.

By now the people in the house had understood we must make a decision. Did we want another cat? We already had two beautiful, large, lazy, neutered toms, who had always had it so good they believed that food, comfort, warmth, safety were what life owed them, for they never had had to fight for anything. No, we did not want another cat, and certainly not a sick one. But now we took out food as well as water to this old derelict, putting it on the balcony so he would know this was a favour and not a right, and that he did not belong to us, and could not come into the house. We joked that he was our outdoor cat.

The hot weather went on.

He ought to be taken to the vet. But that would mean he was our cat, we would have three cats, and our own were being huffy and wary and offended because of this newcomer who seemed to have rights over us, even if limited ones. Besides, what about the old woman whom he did sometimes visit? We watched him go stiffly along a path, turn right to crawl under a fence, cross a garden and then another, his orangeness brilliant against the dulling grass of late summer, and then he vanished and was presumably at the back door of a house where he was welcome.

The hot weather ended and it began to rain. The orange cat stood out in the rain on the balcony, his fur streaked dark with running water, and looked at me. I opened the kitchen door and he came in. I said to him, he could use this chair, but only this chair; this was his chair, and he must not ask for more. He climbed on to the chair and lay down and looked steadily at me. He had the air of one who knows he must make the most of what Fate offers before it is withdrawn.

When it was not raining the door was still open on to the balcony, the trees, the garden. We hate shutting it all out with glass and curtains. And he could still use the lilac tree to get down into the garden for his toilet. He lay all that day on the chair in the kitchen, sometimes getting clumsily off it to drink yet another bowl of water. He was eating a lot now. He could not pass a food or water bowl without eating or drinking something, for he knew he could never take anything for granted.

This was a cat who had had a home, but lost it. He knew what it was to be a house cat, a pet. He wanted to be caressed. His story was a familiar one. He had had a home, human friends who loved him, or thought they did, but it was not a good home because the people went away a lot and left him to find food and shelter for himself, or who looked after him as long as it suited them and then left the neighbourhood, abandoning him. For some time he had been fed at the old woman's place but, it seemed, not enough, or had not been given water to drink. Now he was looking better. But he was not cleaning himself. He was stiff, of course, but he had been demoralized, hopeless. Perhaps he had believed he would never have a home again? After a few days, when he knew we would not throw him out of the kitchen, he began to purr whenever we came into it. Never have I, or anyone else who visited the house, heard any cat purr as loudly as he did. He lay on the chair and his sides went up and down and his purring rumbled through the house. He wanted us to know he was grateful. It was a calculated purr.

We brushed him. We cleaned his fur for him. We gave him a name. We took him to the vet, thus acknowledging that we had a third cat. His kidneys were bad. He had an ulcer in one ear. Some of his teeth had gone. He had arthritis or rheumatism. His heart could be better. But no, he was not an old cat, probably eight or nine years old, in his prime if he had been looked after, but he had been living as he could, and perhaps for some time. Cats who have to scavenge and cadge and sleep out in bad weather in the big cities do not live long. He would soon have died if we had not rescued him. He took his antibiotics and the vitamins, and soon after his first visit to the vet began the painful process of cleaning himself. But parts of himself he was too stiff to reach, and he had to labour and struggle to be a clean and civilized cat.

All this went on in the kitchen, and mostly on the chair, which he was afraid of leaving. His place. His little place. His toehold on life. And when he went out on to the balcony he watched us all in case we shut the door on him, for he feared being locked out more than anything, and if we made movements that looked as if the door might be shutting he scrambled painfully in and on to his chair.

He liked to sit on my lap and, when this happened, he set himself in motion, purring, and he looked up with those clever greyish-yellow eyes: Look, I am grateful, and I am telling you so.

One day, when the arbiters of his fate were in the kitchen drinking tea, he hopped off his chair and walked slowly to the door into the rest of the house. There he stopped and turned and most deliberately looked at us. He could not have asked more clearly: Can I go further into the house? Can I be a proper house cat? By now we would have been happy to invite him in, but our other two cats seemed able to tolerate him if he stayed where he was, a kitchen cat. We pointed to his chair and he climbed patiently back on to it, where he lay silent and disappointed for a while, and then set his sides heaving in a purr. Needless to say, this made us feel terrible.

A few days later, he got carefully off his chair and went to the same door and stopped there, looking back at us for directions. This time we did not say he must come back, so he went on into the house, but not far. He found a sheltered place under a bath and that was where he stayed. The other cats went to check where he was, and enquired of us what we thought of it, but what we thought was, these two young princes could share their good fortune. Outside the house it was autumn, and then winter, and we needed to shut the kitchen door. But what about this new cat's lavatory problems? These days he waited at the kitchen door when he needed to go out, but once there he did not want to jump down on to the little roof, or climb down the lilac tree, for he was too stiff. He used the pots the plants were trying to grow in, so I put down a big box filled with peat, and he understood and used it. A nuisance, having to empty the peat box. There is a cat door right at the bottom of the house into the garden, and our two young cats had never, not once, made a mess inside the house. Come rain or snow or high winds, they go out.

And so that was the situation as winter began. In the evenings people and the two resident cats, the rightful cats, were in the sitting-room, and Rufus was under the bath. And then, one evening, Rufus appeared in the doorway of the sitting-room and it was a dramatic apparition, for here was the embodiment of the dispossessed, the insulted, the injured, making himself felt by the warm, the fed, the privileged. He glanced at the two cats who were his rivals, but kept his intelligent eyes on us. What were we going to say? We said, Very well, he could use the old leather beanbag near the radiator , the warmth would help his aching bones. We made a hollow in the beanbag and he climbed into the hollow and curled up, but carefully, and he purred. He purred, he purred, he purred so loudly and so long we had to beg him to stop, for we could not hear ourselves speak. Literally. We had to turn up the television. But he knew he was lucky and wanted us to know he understood the value of what he was getting. When I was at the top of the house, two floors up, I could hear the rhythmic rumbling that meant Rufus was awake and telling us of his gratitude. Or perhaps he was asleep and purring in his sleep, for once he had started he did not stop but lay there curled up, eyes shut, his sides pumping up and down. There was something inordinate

and scandalous about Rufus's purring, because it was so calculated. And we were reminded, as we watched, and listened to this old survivor, who was only alive now because he had used his wits, of the hazards and adventures and hardships he had undergone.

But our other two cats were not pleased. One is called Charles, originally Prince Charlie, not after the present holder of that title, but after earlier romantic princes for he is a dashing and handsome tabby who knows how to present himself. About his character the less said the better – but this chronicle is not about Charles. The other cat, the older brother, with the character of one, has a full ceremonial name, bestowed when he first left kittenhood and his qualities had become evident. We called him General Pinknose the Third, paying tribute and perhaps reminding ourselves that even the best looked-after cat is going to leave you. We had seen that ice-cream-pink tinge, but on the tips of noses with a less noble curve, on earlier, less imposing cats. Like some people he acquires new names as time makes its revelations, and recently, because of his moral force and his ability to impose silent judgements on a scene, he became for a time a bishop and was known as Bishop Butchkin. Reserving comment, these two cats lay in their respective places, noses on their paws, and watched Rufus. Charles is always under a radiator, but Butchkin likes the top of a tall basket where he can keep an eye on things. He is a magnificent cat. Familiarity had dulled my eyes: I knew he was handsome, but I came back from a trip somewhere to be dazzled by this enormous cat boldly patterned in his shining black and immaculate white, yellow-eyed, with white whiskers, and I thought that this beauty had been bred out of common-or-garden mog-material by good feeding and care. Left unneutered, a cat who had to roam around in all weathers to compete for a mate, he would not look like this, but would be a smaller, or at least gaunt, rangy, war-bitten cat. No, I am not happy about neutering cats, far from it.

But this tale is not about El Magnifico, the name that suits him best.

When he thought we didn't know, Charles would try to get Rufus into a corner and threaten him. But Charles has never had to fight and compete, and Rufus has, all his life. Rufus was so rickety he could be knocked over by the swipe of a determined paw. But he sat back and defended himself with hard experienced stares, with his wary patience, his indomitability. There was no doubt what would happen to Charles if he got within hitting distance. As for El Magnifico, he was above competing on this level.

During all those early weeks, while he was recovering strength, Rufus never went out of the house, except to the peat box on the balcony, and there he did his business, keeping his gaze on us and even now, if it seemed the door might shut him out, he gave a little grunt of panic and then hobbled back indoors. He was so afraid, even now, he might lose this refuge gained after long homelessness, after such torments of thirst. He was afraid to put a paw outside.

The winter slowly went by. Rufus lay in his beanbag and purred every time he thought of it, and he watched us, and watched the two other cats watching him. Then he made a new move. By now we knew he never did anything without very good reason, that first he worked things out, and then acted. The black and white cat, Butchkin, is the boss cat. He was born in this house, one of six kittens. He brought up his siblings as much as his mother did; she was not a bad mother so much as an exhausted one. There was never any question about who was the boss kitten of the litter. Now Rufus decided to make a bid for the position of boss cat. Not by strength, because he did not have that, but by using his position as a sick cat, given so much attention. Every evening The

General, El Magnifico Butchkin, came to lie by me on the sofa for a while, to establish his right to this position, before going to his favourite place on top of the basket. This place by me was the best place, because Butchkin thought it was. Charles, for instance, was not allowed it. But now, just as he had walked deliberately to the kitchen door and then looked back to see if we would allow him to the house itself, just as he had stood in the sitting-room door to find out if we would let him in to join the family, so now Rufus deliberately stepped down off the beanbag, came to where I sat, pulled himself up, first front legs, and then, with difficulty, his back legs and sat down beside me. He looked at Butchkin. Then at the humans. Finally, a careless look at Charles. I did not throw him off. I could not. Butchkin only looked at him and then slowly (and magnificently) yawned. I felt it was he who should make Rufus return to the beanbag. But he did nothing, only watched. Was he waiting for me to act? Rufus lay down, carefully, because of his painful joints. And purred. All people who live with animals have moments when they long to share a language. And this was one. What had happened to him, how had he learned to plan and calculate, how had he become such a thinking cat? All right, so he was born intelligent, but then so was Butchkin, and so was Charles. (And there are very stupid cats.) All right, so he was born with such and such a nature. But I have never known a cat so capable of thought, of planning his next move, as Rufus.

Lying beside me, having achieved the best place in the sitting-room after only a few weeks from being an outcast, he purred. 'Shhh Rufus, we can't hear ourselves think.' But we did not share a language, could not explain that we would not throw him out if he stopped purring, saying thank you.

When we made him swallow pills he made little grunts of protest; he probably saw this as the price he had to pay for a refuge. Sometimes, when we swabbed his ear and it hurt, he swore, but not at us; it was a generally directed curse from one who had much occasion to use curses. Then he licked our hands to show he didn't mean us, and set his purr going again. We stroked him and he gave his rusty grunt of acknowledgement.

Meanwhile, Butchkin the Magnificent watched and thought his own thoughts. His character had a lot to do with Rufus's fate. He is too proud to compete. If he is in intimate conversation with me at the top of the house, and Charles comes in, he simply jumps down off the bed or chair and goes off downstairs. He will not only not tolerate competition felt to be unworthy of him, he won't put up with thoughts not centred on him. Holding him, stroking him, I have to keep my thoughts on him. No such thing, with Butchkin, as stroking him while I read. The moment my thoughts have wandered, he knows it and jumps down and is off. But he doesn't bear grudges. When Charles behaves badly, tormenting him, he might give him a swipe, but then bestows a forgiving lick, *noblesse oblige*.

Such a character is not going to lower himself by fighting any cat for first place.

One day I was standing in the middle of the room addressing myself to Butchkin who was curled on his basket top, when Rufus got down off the sofa and came to stand just in front of my legs, looking at Butchkin as if to say, She prefers me. This was done slowly and deliberately, he was not being emotional or rash or impulsive, all qualities that Charles had too much of. He had planned it, was calm and thoughtful. He had decided to make a final bid to be top cat, my favourite, with Butchkin in second place. But I wasn't going to have this. I pointed at the sofa and he looked up at me in a way which, had he been human, would have said, well, it was worth having a go. And he went back to the sofa.

Butchkin had noted my decisiveness in his favour and did not remark on it more than by getting down off his place, coming to wind himself around my legs, and then going back again.

Rufus had made his bid to be first cat, and failed.

He had not put a paw downstairs for months, but now I saw him trying a clumsy jump on to the roof, and there he looked back, still afraid I might not let him back in, then he eyed the lilac tree, working out how to get down it. Spring had come. The tree was freshly green and the flowers, still in bud, hung in whitish-green fronds. He decided against the tree and jumped painfully back up to the balcony. I picked him up, carried him downstairs, showed him the cat door. He was terrified, thinking it was a trap. I gently pushed him through while he swore and struggled. I went out after him, picked him up, and pushed him back. At once he scrambled up the stairs, thinking I wanted to throw him out altogether. This performance was repeated on successive days and Rufus hated it. In between I petted and praised him so he would know I was not trying to get rid of him.

He thought it over. I saw him get up from his place on the sofa and slowly go down the stairs. He went to the cat door. There he stood, his tail twitching in indecision, examining it. He was afraid; fear drove him back. He made himself stop, return ... several times he did this, then reached the flap itself, and tried to force himself to jump through it, but his instincts rose up in him and forced him away. Again and again this was repeated. And then he made himself do it. Like a person jumping into the deep end, he pushed his head through, then his body, and was in the garden that was full of the scents and sounds of spring, birds jubilating because they had made it through another winter, children reclaiming their playgrounds. The old vagabond stood there, snuffing the air which seemed to fill him with new life, one paw raised, turning his head to catch the smell-messages (what someone in the house calls smellograms) that brought him reminders of former friends, both feline and human, brought him memories. Easy then to see him as a young cat, handsome and full of vigour. Off he went in his deliberate way, limping a little, to the end of the garden. Under the old fruit trees he looked to the right and he looked to the left. Memories tugged him both ways. He went under the fence to the right, in the direction of the old woman's house – or so we supposed. There he stayed for an hour or so, and then I watched him squeezing his way back under the fences into our garden, and he came back down the path and stood at the back door by the cat flap and looked up at me: Please open it, I've had enough for one day. I gave in and opened the door. But next day he made himself go out through the flap, and he came back through the flap, and after that there was no need for a cat box, not even when it rained or snowed or the garden was full of wind and noise. Not, that is, unless he was ill and too weak.

Most often he went visiting to the right, but sometimes off to the left, a longer journey, and I watched him through binoculars, till I lost him in the shrubs. When he returned from either trip he always came at once to be petted, and he set his purring machinery in motion ... it was then we realized his purring was no longer the very loud, insistent, prolonged noise it had been when he first came. Now he purred adequately, with moderation, as befitted a cat who wanted us to be sure he valued us and his place with us, even though he was not top cat and we would not give him first place. For a long time he had been afraid we would prove capricious and throw him out, or lock him out, but now he felt more secure. But at that stage he never went visiting without coming at once to one of us, and purring, and sitting by our legs, or pushing his forehead against us, which meant he would like his ears rubbed, particularly the sore one which would not heal.

That spring and summer were good for Rufus. He was well, as far as he could be. He was sure of us, even though once I incautiously picked up an old broom handle, which lay on the back porch, and I saw him jump down on to the roof, falling over, and he scrambled down the tree and was at the end of the garden in one wild panicky rush. Someone in the past had thrown sticks at him, had beaten him. I ran down into the garden and found him terrified, hiding in a bush. I picked him up, brought him back, showed him the harmless broom handle, apologized, petted him. He understood it was a mistake.

Rufus made me think about the different kinds of cat intelligence. Before that I had recognized that cats had different temperaments. His is the intelligence of the survivor. Charles has the scientific intelligence, curious about everything, human affairs, the people who come to the house, and, in particular, our gadgets. Tape recorders, a turning gramophone table, the television, a radio, fascinate him. You can see him wondering why a disembodied human voice emerges from a box. When he was a kitten, before he gave up, he used to stop a turning record with a paw ... release it ... stop it again ... look at us, miaow an enquiry. He would walk to the back of the radio set to find out if he could see what he heard, go behind the television set, turn over a tape recorder with his paw, sniff at it, miaow, What is this? He is the talkative cat. He talks you down the stairs and out of the house, talks you in again and up the stairs, he comments on everything that happens. When he comes in from the garden you can hear him from the top of the house. 'Here I am at last,' he cries, 'Charles the adorable, and how you must have missed me! Just imagine what has happened to me, you'll never believe it ...' Into the room you are sitting in he comes, and stands in the doorway, his head slightly on one side, and waits for you to admire him. 'Am I not the prettiest cat in this house?' he demands, vibrating all over. Winsome, that's the word for Charles.

The General has his intuitive intelligence, knowing what you are thinking and what you are going to do next. He is not interested in science, how things work; he does not bother to impress you with his looks. He talks when he has something to say and only when he is alone with you 'Ah,' he says, finding that the other cats are elsewhere, 'so we are alone at last.' And he permits a duet of mutual admiration. When I come back from somewhere he rushes from the end of the garden, crying out, 'There you are, I've missed you! How could you go away and leave me for so long?' He leaps into my arms, licks my face and, unable to contain his joy, rushes all over the house like a kitten. Then he returns to being his grave and dignified self.

By the time autumn began Rufus had been behaving like a strong, well cat for some months, visiting friends, sometimes staying away for a day or two. But then he did not go out, he was a sick cat and lay in a warm place, a sad cat with sores on his paws, shaking his head because of the ulcer in his ear, drinking, drinking ... Back to the vet. Verdict: not good, very bad, in fact, sores like these a bad sign. More antibiotics, more vitamins, and Rufus should not go out in the cold and wet. For months Rufus made no attempt to go out. He lay near the radiator, and his hair came out in great thick rusty wads. Wherever he lay, even for a few minutes, was a nest of orange hair, and you could see his skin through the thin fur. Slowly, he got better.

By ill luck it happened that another cat, not ours, needed medicating at the same time. It got itself run over, had a serious operation and convalesced in our house being fussed over and our own two cats did not like it, and took themselves off into the garden away from the upsetting sight. And then Butchkin too seemed ill. When I went into the garden or the sitting-room he was stretching out his neck and coughing in a delicate but gloomy way, suffering nobly borne. I took him to the vet, but there was nothing wrong. A mystery. He went on coughing. In the garden I could not pick up a trowel or pull out a weed without hearing hoarse and hollow coughing. Very odd indeed. One day, when I had petted poor Butchkin and enquired after his health, and given up, and come indoors, I was struck by unpleasant suspicion. I went to the top of the house and watched him through the binoculars. Not a sign of coughing, he was stretched out enjoying the early spring sunlight. Down I went into the garden and, when he saw me, he got into a crouching position, his throat extended, coughing and suffering. I returned to the balcony with the spy glass, and there he lay, his beautiful black and white coat a-dazzle in the sun, yawning. Luckily, the second sick cat recovered and went off to his new home and we were again a three-cat family. Butchkin's cough mysteriously disappeared, and he acquired another name: for a time he was known as Sir Laurence Olivier Butchkin.

Now all three cats enjoyed the garden in their various ways, but pursued in it three parallel existences; if their paths crossed they politely ignored each other.

One sunny morning I saw two orange cats on the fresh grass of the next-door lawn. One was Rufus. His fur had grown back, but thinner than before. He sat firmly upright, confronting a very young male cat who was challenging him. This cat was bright orange, like an apricot in sunlight, a plumy, feathery cat who made delicate jabs, first with one paw and then the other, not actually touching Rufus but, or so it looked, aiming at an imaginary or invisible cat just in front of Rufus. This lovely young cat seemed to be dancing as it sat, it wavered and sidled and patted and prodded the air, and the foxfire shine of its fur made Rufus look dingy. They were alike; this was Rufus's son, I was sure, and in him I was seeing the poor old ragbag Rufus as he had been before the unkindness of humans had done him in. The scene went on for minutes, half an hour. As male cats often do, they seemed to be staging a joust or duel as a matter of form, with no intention of actually hurting each other. The young cat did let out a yowl or two, but Rufus remained silent, sitting solidly on his bottom. The young cat went on feinting with his fringed red paws, then stopped and hastily licked his side as if losing interest in the business, but then, reminded by Rufus's stolid presence that he had an obligation to fight Rufus, he sat up again, all style and pose, like an heraldic cat, a feline on a coat of arms, and resumed his feinting dance. Rufus continued to sit, neither fighting nor refusing to fight. The young cat got bored and wandered off down the garden, prancing at shadows, rolling over and lolling on the grass, chasing insects. Rufus waited until he had gone, and then set off in his quiet way in the direction he was going, this spring, not to the right, to the old lady, but to the left where he might stay hours or even overnight. For he was well again and it was spring, mating time. When he came home he was hungry and thirsty, and that meant he was not making human friends. But then, as spring went on, he stayed longer, perhaps two days, three. He had, I was pretty sure, a cat friend.

Tetchy and petulant Grey Cat had been unfriendly with other cats. Before she was spayed she was unloving with her mates and hostile even to cats living a long time in the same house. She did not have cat friends, only human friends. When she became friendly with a cat for the first time she was old, about thirteen. I was living then in a small flat at the top of a house that had no cat doors, only a staircase to the front door. From there she made her way to the garden at the back of the house. She could push the door open to come in, but had to be let out. She began admitting an old grey cat who would ascend the stairs just behind her, then wait at the door to our flat for her to say he could come up further, and waited at the top to be invited into my room: waited for her invitations, not mine. She liked him. For the first time she was liking a cat who had not begun as her kitten. He would advance quietly into my room – her room, as he saw it – and then went towards her. At first she sat facing him with her back to a big old chair for protection; she wasn't going to trust anyone, not she! He stopped a short way from her and softly miaowed. When she gave a hasty, reluctant mew in reply – for she had become like an old woman who is querulous and bad tempered, but does not know it – he crouched down a foot or so away from her, and looked steadily at her. She too crouched down. They might stay like that for an hour, two hours.

Later she became more relaxed about it all, and they sat crouched side by side, close but not touching. They did not converse, except for soft little sounds of greeting. They liked each other, wanted to sit together. Who was he? Where did he live? I never found out. He was old, a cat who had not had an easy life, for he came up in your hands like a shadow, and his fur was lustreless. But he was a whole cat, a gentlemanly old cat, grey with white whiskers, polite, courtly, not expecting special treatment or, indeed, anything much from life. He would eat a little of her food, drink some milk if offered some, but did not

135

seem hungry. Often when I came back from somewhere he was waiting at the outside door and he miaowed a little, very softly, looking up at me, then came in after me, followed me up the stairs to the door of our flat, miaowed again, and came up the final stairs to the top where he went straight to Grey Cat who let out her cross little miaow when she saw him, but then permitted him a trill of welcome. He spent long evenings with her. She was a changed cat, less prickly and ready to take offence. I used to watch the two of them sitting together like two old people who don't need to talk. Never in my life have I so badly wanted to share a language with an animal. 'Why this cat?' I wanted to ask her. 'Why this cat and no other cat? What is it in this old polite cat that makes you fond of him? For I suppose you will admit you are? All these fine cats in the house, all your life, and you've never liked one of them, but now....'

One evening, he did not come. Not the next. Grey Cat waited for him. She sat watching the door all evening. Then she waited downstairs at the door into the house. She searched the garden. But he did not come, not ever again. And she was never again friends with a cat. Another cat, a male cat who visited the cat downstairs, took refuge with us when he became ill, a few weeks before he died, and lived out the end of his life in my room – her room; but she never acknowledged his existence. She behaved as if only I and she were there.

I believed that Rufus had such a friend, and that was where he was going off to visit.

One evening in late summer he stayed on the sofa by me, and he was there next morning in exactly the same position. When at last he got down, he walked holding up a limp and dangling back leg. The vet said he had been run over: one could tell by his claws, for cats instinctively extend their claws to grip when the wheel drags at them. His claws were broken and split. He had a bad fracture of a back leg.

The cast went on from his ankle to the top of his thigh, and he was put into a quiet room with food and water and a dirt box. There he was happy to stay overnight, but then wanted to come out. We opened the door and watched him clumsily descend the stairs, flight after flight, to the bottom of the house where he swore and cursed as he manoeuvred that sticking-out leg through the cat door, then hopped and hobbled up the path, and swore a lot more as he edged himself and the leg under a fence. Off to the left, to his friend. He was away for about half an hour; he had been to report to someone, feline or human, about his mishap. When he came back, he was pleased to be put back into his refuge. He was shaken, shocked, and his eyes showed he was in pain. His fur, made healthy by summer and good feeding, looked harsh, and he was again a poor old cat who could not easily clean himself. Poor old ragbag! Poor Calamity Cat! He accumulated names as Butchkin does, but they were sad ones. But he was indomitable. He set himself to the task of removing his cast, succeeded, and was returned to the vet to have another put on, which he could not take off. But he tried. And, everyday he made his trip down the stairs, to the cat door, where he hesitated, his leg stuck out behind him, then went through it cursing, because he always knocked his leg on it, and we watched him hobble up the garden through the puddles and leaves of the autumn. He had to lie almost flat to get under the fence. Every day he went to report, and came back exhausted and went to sleep. When awake, he laboured at the task of getting his cast off. Where he sat was white with bits of cast.

In a month it came off, the leg was stiff but usable, and Rufus became himself, a gallant adventuring cat who used us as a base, but then got ill again. For a couple of years this cycle went on. He got well, and was off, got ill and came home. But his illnesses were getting worse. His ear ulcer would not heal. He would return from somewhere to ask for help. He would put his paw delicately to his suppurating ear, retch delicately at the smell on his paw, and look helplessly at his nurses. He gave little grunts of protest as we washed it out, but he wanted us to, and he took his medicaments, and he lay around and allowed himself to get well. Under our hands his was a tough, muscled body and he was a strong old cat, in spite of his ailments. It was only at the end of his life, his much too short life, when he was ill and could hardly walk, that he stayed home and did not attempt to go out at all. He lay on the sofa and seemed to think, or dream, when he was not asleep. Once, when he was asleep, I stroked him awake to take his medicine, and he came up out of sleep with the confiding, loving trill greeting cats use for the people they love, the cats they love. But when he saw it was me he became his normal polite and grateful self, and I realized that this was the only time I had heard him make this special sound – in a house where it was heard all day. This is how mother cats greet their kittens, kittens greet their mothers. Had he been dreaming of when he was a kitten? Or perhaps even of the human who had owned him as a kitten, or a young cat, but then had gone off and abandoned him? I was shocked, and hurt, by this ultimate sound, for he had not made it even when he was purring like a machine to show gratitude. During all the time he had known us, nearly four years, several times nursed back to health, or near-health, he had never really believed he could not lose this home and have to fend for himself, become a cat maddened by thirst and aching with cold. His confidence in someone, his love, had once been so badly betrayed that he could not allow himself ever to love again.

Knowing cats, a lifetime of cats, what is left is a sediment of sorrow quite different from that due to humans: compounded of pain for their helplessness, of guilt on behalf of us all.

White House Cat

THEODORE ROOSEVELT

President Theodore Roosevelt wrote to his son, Kermit,
describing the amusing antics of the boy's kitten,
Tom Quartz.

White House, 6th January 1903

Dear Kermit,

We felt very melancholy after you and Ted left and the
house seemed empty and lonely. But it was the greatest
possible comfort to feel that you both really have
enjoyed school and are both doing well there.

Tom Quartz is certainly the cunningest kitten I have
ever seen. He is always playing pranks on Jack and I get
very nervous lest Jack should grow too irritated. The
other evening they were both in the library – Jack
sleeping before the fire – Tom Quartz scampering about,
an exceedingly playful little creature – which is about
what he is. He would race across the floor, then jump
upon the curtain or play with the tassel. Suddenly he
spied Jack and galloped up to him. Jack, looking
exceedingly sullen and shame-faced, jumped out of the
way and got upon the sofa and around the table, and
Tom Quartz instantly jumped upon him again. Jack
suddenly shifted to the other sofa, where Tom Quartz
again went after him. Then Jack started for the door,

while Tom made a rapid turn under the sofa and around the table and just as Jack reached the door leaped on his hind-quarters. Jack bounded forward and away and the two went tandem out of the room – Jack not co-operating at all; and about five minutes afterwards Tom Quartz stalked solemnly back.

Another evening, the next Speaker of the House, Mr Cannon, an exceedingly solemn, elderly gentleman with chin whiskers, who certainly does not look to be of playful nature, came to call upon me. He is a great friend of mine, and we sat talking over what our policies for the session should be until about eleven o'clock and when he went away I accompanied him to the head of the stairs. He had gone about half-way down when Tom Quartz strolled by, his tail erect and very fluffy. He spied Mr Cannon going down the stairs, jumped to the conclusion that he was a playmate escaping, and raced after him, suddenly grasping him by the leg the way he does Archie and Quentin when they play hide and seek with him; then loosening his hold he tore downstairs ahead of Mr Cannon, who eyed him with an iron calm and not one particle of surprise....

From

Wild Wales

GEORGE BORROW

As I and my family sat at tea in our parlour, an hour or two after we had taken possession of our lodgings, the door of the room and that of the entrance of the house being open, on account of the fineness of the weather, a poor black cat entered hastily, sat down on the carpet by the table, looked up towards us, and mewed piteously. I never had seen so wretched a looking creature. It was dreadfully, attenuated, being little more than skin and bone, and was sorely afflicted with an eruptive malady. And here I may as well relate the history of this cat previous to our arrival which I subsequently learned by bits and snatches. It had belonged to a previous vicar of Llangollen, and had been left behind at his departure. His successor brought with him dogs and cats, who, conceiving that the late vicar's cat had no business at the vicarage, drove it forth to seek another home, which, however, it could not find. Almost all the people of the suburb were dissenters, as indeed were the generality of the people at Llangollen, and knowing the cat to be a church cat, not only would not harbour it, but did all they could to make it miserable; whilst the few who were not dissenters, would not receive it into their houses, either because they had cats of their own, or dogs, or did not want a cat, so that the cat had no home and was dreadfully persecuted by nine-tenths of the suburb. Oh, there never was a cat so persecuted as that poor Church of England animal, and solely on account of the opinions which it was supposed to have imbibed in the house of its late master, for I never could learn that the dissenters of the suburb, nor indeed of Llangollen in general, were in the habit of persecuting other cats; the cat was a Church of England cat, and that was enough: stone it, hang it, drown it! were the cries of almost everybody. If the workmen of the flannel factory, all of whom were Calvinistic Methodists, chanced to get a glimpse of it in the road from the windows of the building, they would sally forth in a body, and with sticks, stones, or for want of other weapons, with clots of horse-dung, of which there was always plenty on the road, would chase it up the high bank or perhaps over the Camlas – the inhabitants of a small street between our house and the factory leading from the road to the river, all of whom were dissenters, if they saw it moving about the perllan, into which their back windows looked, would shriek and hoot at it, and fling anything of no value, which came easily to hand, at the head or body of the ecclesiastical cat. The good woman of the house, who though a very excellent person, was a bitter dissenter, whenever she saw it upon her ground or heard it was there, would make after it, frequently attended by her maid Margaret, and her young son, a boy, about nine years of age, both of whom hated the cat, and were always ready to attack it, either alone or in company, and no wonder, the maid being not only a dissenter, but a class teacher, and the boy not only a dissenter, but intended for the dissenting ministry. Where it got its food, and food it sometimes must have got, for even a cat, an animal known to have nine lives, cannot live without food, was only known to itself, as was the place where it lay, for even a cat must lie down sometimes; though a labouring man who occasionally dug in the garden told me he believed that in the springtime it ate freshets, and the woman of the house once said that she believed it sometimes slept in the hedge, which hedge, by the bye, divided our perllan from the vicarage grounds, which were very extensive. Well might the cat, having led this kind of life for better than two years, look mere skin and bone when it made its appearance in our apartment, and have an eruptive malady, and also a bronchitic cough, for I remember it had both. How it came to make its appearance there is a mystery, for it had never entered the house before, even when there were lodgers; that it should not visit the woman, who was its declared enemy, was natural enough, but why, if it did not visit her other lodgers, did it visit us? Did instinct keep it aloof from them? Did instinct draw it towards us? We gave it some bread-and-butter, and a little tea with milk and sugar. It ate and drank and soon began to purr. The good woman of the house was horrified when on coming in to remove the things she saw the church cat on her carpet. 'What impudence!' she exclaimed, and made towards it, but on our telling her that we did not expect that it should be disturbed, she let it alone. A very remarkable circumstance was, that though the cat had hitherto been in the habit of flying not only from her face, but the very echo of her voice, it now looked her in the face with perfect composure, as much as to say, 'I don't fear you, for I know that I am now safe and with my own people.' It stayed with us two hours and then went away. The next morning it returned. To be short, though it went away every night, it became our own cat, and one of our family. I gave it something which cured it of its eruption, and through good treatment it soon lost its other ailments and began to look sleek and bonny.

We were at first in some perplexity with respect to the disposal of the ecclesiastical cat; it would of course not do to leave it in the garden to the tender mercies of the Calvinistic Methodists of the neighbourhood, more especially those of the flannel manufactory, and my wife and daughter could hardly carry it with them. At length we thought of applying to a young woman of sound church principles who was lately married and lived over the water on the way to the railway station, with whom we were slightly acquainted, to take charge of the animal, and she on the first intimation of our wish willingly acceded to it. So with her poor puss was left along with a trifle for its milk-money, and with her, as we subsequently learned, it continued in peace and comfort till one morning it sprang suddenly from the hearth into the air, gave a mew and died. So much for the ecclesiastical cat.

Cat Burglars

JACQUIE WINES

In the time that they lived there, Senior and Junior became the most notorious cats in Nelson Road. Nobody knows from where they came, or to whom they belonged, but both turned up within weeks of each other at the home of Iris and Ken Weston. Iris and Ken preferred dogs – indeed they owned a dog, Fred, who had been part of their family for many years.

However, when first the shabby ginger cat, followed by the sleeker tortoiseshell arrived at their home, and when, in spite of their best efforts, no one came forward to claim them, the couple didn't have the heart to turn them out on to the mercy of the street. Now these cats were well-fed. Not only did Iris and Ken feed them on chicken and tuna, but they also gave them the leftovers of their meals. Poor Fred rarely seemed to get a look in. Neither were the cats shy of stealing food from his bowl, and with a little swiping, digging of claws and collective hissing, they soon had the poor dog at their mercy.

A few months after the cats took up residence, Iris noticed a pair of strange socks in her laundry basket. Ken confirmed that they did not belong to him, but the couple really thought no more of it until, a few days later, they found themselves in possession of two bras and a large pair of men's pants. The following day Iris found a

145

baby's shoe, a man's shirt, and a small teddy bear in the basket. Bemused, they put the laundry basket into the middle of their lawn and spied upon it until they saw Senior emerging over the garden wall with a handkerchief.

Torn between laughter and the thought of what their neighbours must be saying, the couple decided to gather up the items and knock on every street door until they found the owners. Senior could not be dissuaded from his thieving ways, and although most of the neighbours knew to watch out for him, few of them ever claimed the items that found their way into Ken and Iris's house. So, once a year, the couple sold off the items, and the money was put toward Christmas drinks for everyone in Weston Road.

If Senior had a fondness for soft goods, Junior had a penchant for edibles. His first gift to the Weston's was a lamb chop, which he left in Ken Weston's slipper. Shortly afterwards, Iris found a gammon steak on her clean duvet. It was not long before a turkey roll, a chicken carcass and a dressed salmon found their way to the Weston household. Now Junior was a beautiful and friendly cat, but the Westons could not condone his behaviour. They tried holding Junior's nose over each 'present' and gently smacking him, and they reacted very angrily when he brought a new gift into the house. But still the goods arrived.

One Sunday the Westons went for supper at their friends' house, three streets away. The Clarks were keen on fishing and Bob Clark had promised them a particularly fine trout for dinner. They enjoyed crab mousse for starters and were just loosening their belts in anticipation of the next course, when a howl was heard from the kitchen. The trout had vanished. The Westons were as astonished as their neighbours, but politely made do with ham and cheese.

When they arrived home, they were greeted by a fishy

odour in the hall. Lo and behold, there beside the telephone was the vanished trout. The Westons fell about with laughter and, to this day, Bob Clark scratches his head about his lost catch.

Senior spent three happy years helping himself to the pickings of Nelson Road, before developing kidney trouble. The vet also discovered that his stomach contained a quantity of wool. Junior disappeared after a year of fairly intensive thieving, vanishing like the food from the neighbours' plates. It was later discovered that he had got into a farmer's chicken shed, and that the farmer had fired an air rifle at him. Junior escaped, chickenless, but was not seen in Nelson Road again.

The Achievement of the Cat

SAKI

The animal which the Egyptians worshipped as divine, which the Romans venerated as a symbol of liberty, which Europeans in the ignorant Middle Ages anathematized as an agent of demonology, has displayed to all ages two closely blended characteristics – courage and self-respect. No matter how unfavourable the circumstances, both qualities are always to the fore.

Confront a child, a puppy, and a kitten with a sudden danger; the child will turn instinctively for assistance, the puppy will grovel in abject submission to the impending visitation, the kitten will brace its tiny body for a frantic resistance. And disassociate the luxury-loving cat from the atmosphere of social comfort in which it usually contrives to move, and observe it critically under the adverse conditions of civilization – that civilization which can impel a man to the degradation of clothing himself in tawdry ribald garments and capering mountebank dances in the streets for the earning of the few coins that keep him on the respectable, or non-criminal, side of society. The cat of the slums and alleys, starved, outcast, harried, still keeps amid the prowlings of its adversity the bold, free, panther-tread with which it paced of yore the temple courts of Thebes, still displays the self-reliant watchfulness which man has never taught it to lay aside.

And when its shifts and clever managings have not sufficed to stave off inexorable fate, when its enemies have proved too strong or too many for its defensive powers, it dies fighting to the last, quivering with the choking rage of mastered resistance, and voicing in its death-yell that agony of bitter remonstrance which human animals, too, have flung at the powers that may be; the last protest against a destiny that might have made them happy – and has not.

Minna Minna Mowbray

MICHAEL JOSEPH

Among all my cats, past and present, Minna Minna Mowbray was an outstanding personality. Except to a connoisseur of cats Minna was not physically impressive. She was a short-haired tortoiseshell tabby, with tiny white paws to match her piquant white face. Her head was small but beautifully shaped. The rather large ears were grey, and streaks of orange fur ran down between her amber eyes and on either side to the under part of her delicate jaw, forming a regularly designed tortoiseshell frame for her white face. A flash of coral pink was visible when she opened her dainty mouth. Her teeth were white and strong. The under part of her body was pure white and even in the soot and grime of London this was nearly always spotlessly clean. At kitten time it was dazzlingly white. This part of her was domestically known as her 'ermine'. When she was feeling particularly sociable, certain favoured members of the household were permitted, sometimes even encouraged, to massage it gently.

Minna was small, as cats go, but exquisitely proportioned. All her movements were graceful. She would sit upright, with her tiny forepaws close together,

her long, rather full tail coiled round. Her favourite position for sleep was a crouch, the hind legs drawn up close and head resting on the outstretched forepaws which she converted into cushions by turning them inwards. Sometimes she preferred to lie on her side, legs outstretched luxuriously at queer angles. Various attitudes I learned to recognize as meditative (often assumed, this one), ecstatic, proud (both these when kittens were on view), majestically indignant (accompanied by business with tail), enquiring (as when she wanted to know what I was eating – this was primarily curiosity, for as often as not she rejected after close scrutiny the morsel I offered her) and leave-me-alone-please. This last was indicated by a haughty turning aside of her head; if this failed she would calmly turn her back and if *that* gesture had no effect she would walk off with the air of an offended dowager.

Like her mother, Lady Dudley, she had no voice, her vocal chord being partially paralysed. Oddly enough – for such a physical defect is presumably not hereditary – her kittens seldom cried, except when they were very young. Minna opened her mouth when, for instance, she wanted a door open, but no sound emerged. When she was greatly agitated about something a faint squeak was audible if you listened carefully. She could purr loudly enough but did not purr often. She could also swear, in delicate but determined fashion, but this again was reserved for special occasions.

Minna Minna Mowbray was a gentle cat. She never attempted to scratch a human. Babies and small boys could do what they liked with her. Like all self-respecting cats she disliked rough handling but she never attempted retaliation. If her tail were pulled or her long, sensitive whiskers touched she showed displeasure by asking silently to be allowed to go.

Contrary to expert advice, Minna wore a collar – an elegant green collar with an identity disc and two brass bells. A collar, I have heard, is undesirable because it may catch in the spikes of railings or the branches of a tree, but in my experience this risk is negligible if a cat is trained to a collar when very young. It is possible that a grown cat may so resent the introduction of a collar that he will try to drag it off and thereby injure himself, but I have never heard of an instance.

Minna was proud of her collar and plainly enjoyed wearing it. She put the bells to practical use, whenever she wanted to be admitted to a room, by shaking her head outside the closed door. She never worried if she were late for breakfast, knowing that the tinkle of her bell would cause the door to be opened. Sometimes when she rang outside the door I delayed, for the satisfaction of hearing her tinkle imperiously repeated. And with what an air of affronted majesty she stalked into the room if she had been thus kept waiting! Custom brought her to the dining-room at breakfast time, not hunger, for as often as not she turned up her aristocratic nose at the fish or milk offered her.

Minna also learned to summon her kittens by sounding her bells. When the babies got to the exploring stage and escaped from the maternal eye in house or garden Minna recalled them by an agitated peal. They usually answered the summons promptly but Minna would continue to ring until they did.

Minna could silence her bell as effectively as she could ring it. Not a sound was to be heard when she stalked a bird. What a waste of time it is to 'bell the cat' with the intention of suppressing natural instincts!

The real owner of my house in those days was Minna. She walked about with the manner of a landed proprietor surveying his domain; on the whole proud, but reserving the right to be critical. The day nursery and the kitchen were her favourite rooms. The dining-room and what my family insisted on calling `the study.' were frequently patronized. Her appearances in the other rooms were rare, with the exception of my bedroom in the winter when warm milk was usually to be coaxed from me last thing at night.

When she was younger the bathroom enchanted her. She soon discovered it to be a magic, fascinating and deliciously dangerous place with a queer contraption which was often filled with water. As a kitten, Minna used to insist on stalking round the edge of the bath when there was water in it, balancing precariously at the rounded corners. Running water fascinated her and she would play with a dripping tap for hours. Her mother, and some of Minna's own kittens, shared this fondness for running water; and so did my favourite Siamese, Charles. Micky Jos, one of Minna's most spirited kittens, had a passion for water and thoroughly enjoyed being soaked to the skin. But when she was grown up, with matronly responsibilities, Minna seldom played with water. It was beneath her dignity.

Another forsaken attraction in her middle age was the piano. As a kitten she took a great interest in it. As soon as it was opened she would jump on the keyboard. A series of spirited discords marked her progress from bass to treble and back again. She much preferred the bass, possibly because the deeper volume of sound or the stronger vibration took her fancy. But, as she grew up, Minna tired of the piano and took no notice of it.

Minna had a curious aversion to whistling. If I tried to whistle (it is not one of my accomplishments) Minna was at once agitated and tried to stop it by putting her paw on my lips. So long as I continued she behaved as one would expect an operatic tenor to behave within hearing of a mouth organ. It was not often that I outraged Minna's artistic susceptibilities but, when I did, her agitation was intense.

Flowers had a curious attraction for Minna. She could never resist nibbling at them. Spring flowers particularly; if not prevented she would drag daffodils and tulips to the ground for the aesthetic satisfaction of sampling their flavour at her leisure. It was not that she required vegetable diet for grass, which cats eat regularly when they can get it, was easily accessible. Minna's taste for flowers was not utilitarian.

If there was one thing Minna disliked more than any other it was preparation for a journey. As soon as suitcases were produced she made a prompt and plaintive appearance on the scene. Her agitation always increased when packing began. She would sit mournfully looking on while cupboards and drawers shed their contents, every now and then making a timid and reproachful attempt to interfere with our progress. Even the perfunctory packing of a suitcase for a weekend disturbed her. As for the wholesale removal of the family during the summer, that was a terrible ordeal. On one occasion, when boxes and cases were being brushed as a preliminary to their annual excursion, Minna, shaking her bell in protest, disappeared downstairs, to reappear a few minutes later with Peter, our wire-haired terrier. And then the pair of them sat gazing lugubriously at the signs of departure.

Minna, like most cats, disliked travelling. She had a very commodious basket (I was always annoyed by people who called it a dog basket) and entered it with a poor grace. Poor dear, she knew what was coming. However comfortably the basket was lined, the taxi jolted her up and down and the noise of passing traffic frightened her. The ignominy of being deposited on the platform of a railway station was bad enough, but worse was to follow. The train was the climax of her ordeal.

It was only when Minna was with me in a railway carriage that the sensation of being cooped up in a swiftly moving box oppressed me. To the more sensitive creature, who was my cat, the jolting, swaying movement of the small compartment which carried us so swiftly and mysteriously to an unknown destination must have been a paralysing torture. It was only then that I realized how uncomfortable even the most modern railway carriage is. Poor Minna! She would emerge timidly from her basket, grateful for release, but terrified of the unknown. Even in her fear curiosity compelled her to climb for a view of the rushing landscape. A glimpse was enough, and down on to the floor she would spring, crouching and panting, her little tongue hanging from her mouth like a signal of distress.

Only once do I remember Minna facing a railway journey with equanimity – and that, I am sure, was more apparent than real. On that occasion Minna was the proud mother of five kittens, who had also to be transported. The booking-office clerk stared when I told him I had six cats with me. When I added that they were infants in arms and enquired if there were any reduction on account of either age or quantity, or both, he grinned comprehendingly. I was mad, of course. He gave me one ticket and took my half-crown with cheerful tolerance. I betook myself and my cat basket off hastily before he could change his mind.

Minna, evidently determined to conquer her fears for the sake of her kittens, was remarkably self-possessed. She submitted without anxiety to imprisonment in the basket and made no fuss when it was lifted into the taxi and dumped on the floor. Not until the train was speeding southwards and she was allowed the freedom of the carriage did she betray her usual agitation. And then, I observed, only when she was well clear of the basket and its tiny occupants. On the seat beside me, snatching a furtive look out of the window from time to time, Minna went through the familiar performance of crying silently, appealing to me with a troubled paw to bring the dreadful and mysterious train to a standstill. But she had one eye all the time on the basket below and, at the first whimpering sound, she was back again, comforting her babies with soft maternal purring.

Minna was always an exemplary mother. But cats vary considerably in this respect. I have already mentioned Meestah, an earlier kitten of Lady Dudley's and therefore a half-sister to Minna. Meestah was worse than neglectful. Her nomenclature, by the way, was based on an Arab word meaning 'to hide' for she had a strange habit of hiding away in odd corners.

It was so long before Meestah became a mother that we began to think she would escape the destiny of female cats, but one day the family arrived – two beautiful kittens. Meestah was most resentful. She would have nothing to do with them. All our coaxing was of no avail. Fortunately, this was when I had fourteen cats. About nine of them were females and the kittens problem was rapidly becoming serious. But, luckily for Meestah's kittens, another of my large cat family accommodatingly had kittens just then and, as the litter was small, we were able to add Meestah's offspring to the new nursery. This was met with the complete approval of both mothers. Meestah was enormously relieved. That was her sole venture into motherhood. How Minna must have disapproved of her!

Minna adored having kittens. Indeed, a cynical friend once remarked that it was her life's work. Her kittens were invariably beautiful and never commonplace. Tortoiseshell tabby, orange, and prettily marked black and white were the usual arrivals, and there were often black flecked with bronze, and kittens mottled distinctively which I am at a loss to describe. Sometimes they were long-haired but usually they inherited the smooth, short-haired coat of their mother. Lest it be thought that I was prejudiced in their favour I must add that Minna's kittens excited admiration even in people usually indifferent to cats.

The fame of my Minna's kittens spread far and wide. Her offspring grew into handsome cats in households all over the country. As my work brought me into touch

with a large number of authors, several of her kittens were transferred to literary ownership. Other kittens went to more modest family circles. Our milkman was a regular customer. He had been rather unlucky with his kittens and we cheerfully replaced them. The fishmonger begged for one which captivated him; and the little orange tabby which went to the greengrocer's wife was the recipient of so much affection that I am sure he did not begrudge the others the natural advantages of their respective establishments.

Several times we resolved to keep for ourselves a particularly charming kitten. There was Dinah, a fluffy, sentimental and very attractive young lady whom we brought from the country when we went to live in Regent's Park. I was especially fond of Dinah; whenever Minna held herself aloof – and that was often – Dinah could be depended on to stay purring blissfully on my knee. Dinah was as affectionate as she was decorative.

Not long after our arrival in London Dinah was reported missing. The usual frantic search followed, with no result. Dinah's virtues were magnified with the passing days and, when at last I had to admit there was no longer any hope of finding her, my loss seemed irreparable. I can write of my lost Dinah in this lighthearted way on account of what followed.

One Sunday morning, some weeks later, someone looking out of a window said, 'Isn't that Dinah?' I must explain that the back of our house faced the backs of a crescent of other houses, with small gardens abutting on each other. In these gardens were trees and on a low-lying bough there was a cat. It certainly did look like Dinah.

I ran down to the garden and, climbing on to the wall, made my way along until I was close enough to identify the cat. It was Dinah. She watched me coming and when I called her name looked down at me with mild interest. I noticed, with relief, that she had evidently been well fed and cared for. If she recognized me she did not show it. Balancing precariously, I tried to coax her down. Dinah took no notice. So, feeling rather foolish, I retired, in the vain hope that she would follow.

Then I had an inspiration. Dinah might have transferred her affections to another human being, but what about her mother? I dashed into the house, picked up Minna and returned to the garden wall. To reach the tree I had to pass along the tops of several garden walls, on some of which my neighbours had erected trelliswork, wire and such-like impediments. With Minna doing her best to escape it was no easy matter to negotiate these obstacles but, apart from blacking my hands and face and tearing my trousers on a nail, I completed the journey safely. I was confident that Dinah would eagerly come down as soon as she saw Minna; and that Minna would be overjoyed to find her lost baby.

I held Minna up in my arms, balancing on tiptoe, so that the two cats could see each other face to face. Dinah looked down on us with surprise, as if to remark what a strange world this was, with human beings performing antics with other cats on the tops of walls. Her innocent eyes looked at Minna with an expression which clearly said, 'I dont know you, madam, and I don't want to know you.' Minna, on the other hand, recognized her offspring at once. Was she overjoyed? Did she utter the crooning call, half purr, half squeak, with which she had always summoned her kittens? Not she. She spat viciously and began to swear under her breath, in a suppressed note of unmistakable feline hate. She kept it up in a steady crescendo until I lowered her on to the wall and let her go; and then she sprang to the ground, lashing her tail with fury.

At the time I was amazed at this unmotherly behaviour. Dinah was still a kitten and only a few weeks before had been the apple of her mother's eye. It was inconceivable that she could have become a stranger in so short a time. I knew that grown cats fail to recognize their parents, and vice versa, but there was Minna behaving in a way most unnatural and offensive.

Later, I became suspicious. It dawned on me that there was something odd about these disappearances of favourite kittens. Whenever we tried to keep one of a litter, it invariably left us before it was many months old. Everyone who has had anything to do with cats knows how distressed the mother cat is when a kitten is lost or taken away, especially if it is the sole survivor of a litter. Now, it struck me as curious that Minna showed no anxiety when these mysterious departures occurred. We all searched high and low, but Minna was quite unconcerned.

It was when Fowey vanished that my suspicions were confirmed. Fowey (named after the Cornish seaport) was a mischievous orange rascal with china-blue eyes, the throatiest purr I have ever heard, an insatiable appetite and absurd fluffy paws which contrasted oddly with the dainty and aristocratic white feet of his mother. He was an intelligent and charming kitten and everyone made a great fuss of him.

When Fowey was about three months old, Minna took him for long walks. On one occasion I discovered them in a field by the railway a long way from the house. No doubt these expeditions were a source of delight to little Fowey, who wanted to see the world, but there seemed to me to be something sinister about them.

One day mother and son left the house together, Fowey as usual prancing with delight at the prospect of yet another expedition into the fascinating unknown. I watched them go, and there was a queer look in Minna's eye, a look which I can only describe as sinister. Maybe it was only my fancy but it was enough to make me ask at once for Fowey when I returned home that evening. My fears were realized; Minna was there, smirking triumphantly, I fancied, but Fowey was missing.

The days went by and Fowey did not return. We searched in vain. When I asked Minna she looked up at me with an expression so blandly innocent that I am sure she understood perfectly well what I was talking about. Now there is no doubt whatever in my mind that what happened was this. Minna took Fowey to some unfamiliar, deserted spot and there turned round and attacked her unsuspecting offspring. Most probably she said something like this to him:

'Look here, young Fowey *(bang)* you understand this *(scratch)*. I'm the only cat wanted in Their house *(biff)* and I'm not *(scratch)* going to have you on the premises. *(Bite, scratch, bang.)* You go and find a home of your own. *(Spit.)* You're not wanted, d'you hear me? *(Bang, spit, bite, scratch, and general fireworks.)'*

No wonder poor Fowey beat a retreat like all the others! He reappeared a few weeks later in one of the gardens at the back and I discovered that he was lording it over one of the houses in the neighbouring crescent. He had grown into a magnificent cat with a long coat (carefully brushed, I was glad to note) and a huge plume of a tail which I could see daily fluttering in the trees when I was shaving in my bathroom. He was, to judge by appearances, a happy cat and played joyously in the gardens most of the day. But he never came into ours.

Minna was an expert in the art of getting her own way. I can recall only two occasions when she was defeated and then I think she allowed herself to be. The first occasion was the little matter of Peter's basket.

Peter belonged to my wife before I knew her and, incidentally, there were times when that dog made me feel as a second husband must feel when his wife describes the virtues of his predecessor. Who is this interloper? Peter seemed to say. Well, when Peter became part of the new *ménage* the basket came along too, but in the excitement of meeting Minna Minna Mowbray and the consequent revolution in his habits and ideas of home life, Peter apparently forgot about the basket.

My wife was upset. She said that Peter was so intelligent he wouldn't go to sleep anywhere but in his basket. (That was before she knew the change Minna could produce.) So it came about that Peter slept – I suspect uneasily – on the mat outside her bedroom door. Then one day my wife said, 'Poor Peter! No wonder he looks unhappy. He hasn't got his basket.' So the basket was dug out of the pile of miscellaneous kit which was awaiting disposal in the new house, and was ceremoniously put outside the door for Peter's accommodation. I rather liked the look of it and reflected aloud, to my wife's indignation, that Minna Minna Mowbray could just do with a basket like that.

Peter wagged his stump, looked intelligent and barked. That night he occupied the basket according to plan. We knew something was wrong (from Peter's point of view) when he scratched at the door the next morning about an hour before his usual time. He came in with the air of an ill-used dog, his stump registering dejection.

We had not long to wait for the explanation. Shortly after tea Minna Minna Mowbray stalked upstairs and leisurely installed herself in the basket. By the time we turned off the radio and went upstairs to bed she was coiled up fast asleep (or ostensibly so) while Peter, squatting on the landing, regarded her balefully from a discreet distance.

That was the beginning of the basket war. The old Trojan War, the Hundred Years War, and the Great War faded into insignificance. Our household was promptly divided into two factions – the pro-Peterites, led by my wife, and the pro-Minnaites, which was me. The cook thought it was too bad, the parlourmaid echoed, 'Poor Peter.' It is true the postman grinned unsympathetically when he heard about it, but he and Peter are traditional enemies so that he was more anti-Peter than pro-Minna.

The fact that numbers were against her did not daunt

my Minna. Her tiny stature was deceptive. In action she could give points to any Amazon. So that Peter's fugitive attempts to regain possession of his sleeping quarters are scarcely worth recording. Except perhaps the day when, bloated with tea and Dutch courage, he made a spirited attempt to get in while Minna dozed peacefully on the cushion. The battle was swiftly over; Peter emerged from the regions of the coal cellar only after an interval of two days and much coaxing.

Then other and more important domestic affairs took precedence over the Minna-Peter feud. While the rest of the household talked of other things it rumbled on in a state of trench warfare, with Minna securely dug in and Peter making occasional raids across no-man's-landing. Indeed, we all regarded the basket war as a permanent feature of our domestic life.

Actually it lasted for just over two years. Armistice was declared only when our baby daughter Shirley crawled out of the bedroom door, seized Minna by the scruff of her furry neck, neatly ejected her and solemnly climbed into the basket.

Peter was present at the ceremony and (presumably) gave a loud doggy guffaw. Minna withdrew with dignity. She then turned the day nursery into her sleeping quarters and Peter retired to the kitchen. The basket was 'reconstructed' after the war and for a long time was occupied by a teddy bear, a musical duck and a woolly rabbit. There was peace in our time.

The other occasion when Minna graciously surrendered was the advent of Charles O'Malley, my Siamese cat. I have written another book about Charles and I shall not say much about him here; although readers of that book may understand my feeling that this is Hamlet without the Prince of Denmark.

Charles O'Malley was the first Siamese I had had. Minna Minna Mowbray was furious when I brought him home and always looked upon him as an intruder. It was quite clear that she would never forgive me for adopting another cat. As for Charles himself, Minna at first swore and spat vigorously at his approach. But she soon decided to tolerate him and after a fortnight or so the two cats were drinking peaceably from the same saucer. Charles, as a ten-week-old kitten, was enormously impressed by Minna Minna Mowbray. No amount of bad language or threats deterred him from the pursuit of her tail but it was several weeks before Minna permitted him to play with her.

Charles O'Malley was aristocratically bred, and looked it. With his sapphire-blue eyes, delicate cream coat, chocolate-pointed ears, feet, tail and 'mask', he was a truly handsome creature.

There are differences between Siamese and other cats, apart from their shape and colouring. The Siamese voice is quite distinctive. When Minna first heard Charles's raucous squeak she visibly shuddered. Siamese cats have the reputation of being ferocious fighters; they are certainly stronger than ordinary cats. I do not think they are so graceful when walking or jumping. Indeed, Charles would land on his feet with a thud which was positively canine. Siamese are exquisite animals, however; sensitive, intelligent and responsive. Charles O'Malley (whom I confess I adopted partly to annoy Minna, who had been treating me very cavalierly at the

time) was indeed a most lovable and charming cat and, as readers of his story will know, he was destined to become my best loved cat.

However, no despot ever ruled his kingdom with more certainty of getting his own way than Minna Minna Mowbray did the house which we then lived in. It was a benevolent tyranny, this rule of Minna's; often amusing, never malicious, always sure and precise. She was clearly a believer in the divine right of cats, exercising her power with due regard to the niceties and obligations of her position.

To the uninitiated it may appear that I was merely foolish about my cat. However, I was not Minna's only subject. She bossed everyone in the house with the exception of my little daughter, Shirley, who occasionally did a bit of bossing herself. But Minna was quite happy about that. Shirley was privileged to stroke her fur the wrong way, to play with her tail and to carry her round the nursery suspended at all sorts of queer angles. I fancy that Minna rather enjoyed it all. Shirley was very fond of her and if Minna was accidentally hurt when they were playing together – this rarely happened, for Shirley knew she must be careful – the ensuing ceremony of contrite apology on the part of one and gracious forgiveness of the other was delightful to watch.

When Minna had kittens Shirley was a privileged visitor from the time of their birth. Minna allowed her to stroke them, knowing that Shirley would only touch them with gentleness. As soon as the babies reached the romping age Shirley was in her element. The nursery was transformed into an arena, in which young tigers leaped and raced swiftly in all directions, with Shirley's attempts at pursuit interrupted by her gurgles of excited laughter. Minna used to look on quite happily at these performances.

Like all cats who are happily accommodated in a human household Minna was a docile creature. But she insisted on having her own way. She would observe, with well-bred interest, my wife's painstaking preparations to provide her with a comfortable and secluded bed for her kittens. A large cardboard box, of the kind she loved, carefully lined with successive layers of newspaper, tissue paper and soft linen, and placed in one of her favourite cupboards, which was conveniently warm, well ventilated and discreetly dark – this was dutifully prepared at certain times by one of us. Whoever prepared her bed, however comfortably made and conveniently placed it might be, we could be sure of one thing – Minna would not use it.

Minna deceived several generations of interested cooks and house-parlourmaids by her tactics on these occasions. It was her custom to inspect at intervals the box or basket which had been so thoughtfully made ready for her, even to occupy it for forty winks every now and again as if to advertise her satisfaction. Many a beaming domestic servant announced the good news that 'Minnie is very pleased with her new box.' But these premature expectations were invariably disappointed. Minna knew what she was about. The attention of our expectant domestic staff being thus publicly drawn to a particular spot, Minna had her kittens elsewhere.

In this respect most cats, I believe, behave in the same independent way. Is it yet another survival of jungle instinct, this hiding away from prying eyes at important times? Or merely a gesture of independence, a rejection of our human proprietorship, a challenge to man and his stupid ways? Minna, although intensely secretive about her plans, made no further attempt at concealment when her kittens were born. She was then embarrassingly anxious that they should be seen and admired. In this I think she may have differed from other cats who, reasonably enough, do not like to be disturbed for some days. Minna, however, scorned further camouflage. She unmistakably invited us to pay our respects to the new arrivals. Nor did she object to their being touched. Our praise was clearly to her liking; she would purr loudly if we admired the little, squealing, almost invisible babies.

Naturally enough she would resent it if we overstayed our welcome, or if any stranger intruded on her privacy. And what a calamity if there should be any attempt to move her family! In that event, as soon as the coast was clear, Minna would remove them methodically, one by one, to what she obviously trusted would be a place less liable to disturbance. She was quite capable of registering a protest if disturbed by strangers; this usually took the form of depositing her kittens under the cover of my bed. There were times when I arrived home to find the house in a state of agitation because Minna and her kittens had disappeared. Nearly always they were to be found huddled together at the end of my bed comfortably asleep under the warm and sheltering darkness of the eiderdown.

Minna brooked no interference in her private affairs. At an early age she began to take an active interest in the opposite sex and all our well-meant efforts to influence her in the direction of a more lady-like modesty were frustrated. If the doors were shut she climbed out of a window. Nor were our attempts to find her a worthy husband any more successful. Whether the so-called attraction of opposites is responsible or not, it is a lamentable fact that Minna invariably chose the most disreputable gentleman friends. Any ugly, one-eyed, torn-eared tom cat seemed to have an irresistible attraction for our Minna Minna Mowbray.

The uglier they were, the more eligible they appeared to be. She had, I remember, a disgraceful passion for an old roué with a lacerated tail, fractional ears, a permanently closed left eye and a pronounced limp. At his approach Minna behaved in a shameless and otherwise indescribable fashion. On such occasions I used to pretend she was not my cat.

When we were living in Surrey we did our best to reform her. It was not successful. Within a few days of our arrival the news had spread in some mysterious fashion that a new and comely lady cat had taken up her residence and that she had a decided preference for experienced lovers. Somehow Minna had made it known to the cats of all Surrey (and part of Sussex, too, I fancy) that she liked to choose her followers from the ranks of the veterans and middle-aged. She had no use for boy friends, it appeared.

We discovered this, and were considerably humiliated thereby, when we introduced her to a young orange cat from a neighbouring house. As soon as we set eyes on this cat, we decided that here was an ideal husband for Minna. He was a strikingly handsome cat, young and, so far as we could see, perfectly eligible. Minna, however, thought not. She promptly spat at him in a most unlady-like way. Our candidate let us down badly. He fled for his life. After that we left Minna to her own devices – and to the reprobate toms of the neighbourhood.

To look at Minna Minna Mowbray as she sat demurely on the arm of my chair, her little white paws set neatly together in a modest pose, you would never imagine that she favoured the toughs and tramps of the tom cat world. In every other respect she was fastidious to the point of absurdity. She would refuse to drink from a saucer that was not spotlessly clean; would spend hours industriously making her toilet, until every hair was in its proper place; insisted on her milk being at exactly the right temperature; and objected to being touched, making a pretence of exquisite discomfort if I happened to stroke her when she didn't feel like it or to lay hands, however gently, on any part of her sensitive anatomy. Yet, ten minutes later, she could be observed (if you cared to gaze on the unedifying spectacle) in the garden below, being rolled playfully about in the mud by a caveman lover from the slums of Camden Town.

The Worshipful Cat

No written records tell us exactly when or how cats became associated with the Egyptian deities, but it seems not to have taken very long (in historical terms, at least; perhaps around 500 years). Two goddesses, in particular, became associated with cats: Sekhmet, a lion-headed goddess, and Bastet, a cat goddess (also known as Bast or Pasht). They were, at times, considered twins and earlier images of Bastet show her also as having the head of a lion, though later she would always have a cat's head.

Although both goddesses were associated with the sun, Sekhmet was always considered the fiercer of the two, being linked to the strong destructive heat of the desert rays, while Bastet represented the nurturing, life-giving aspect of solar warmth. Because Egyptian deities had a confusing tendency to overlap, fade into each other, or become associated with different ideas in different places, Sekhmet and Bastet sometimes seem interchangeable, depending on time and location.

In her capacity as a sun-goddess, Bastet also represented fertility, motherhood and beauty. Bastet generally is depicted as a woman with the head of a cat, including long, sharply pointed ears. She wears a long, clingy gown and frequently carries a basket, an aegis (a small shield, sometimes bearing the head of a lion) and/or a sistrum (a kind of rattle or musical instrument).

The basket may have kittens in it, the sistrum frequently has cats carved on it, and kittens may be gambolling about the goddess's feet.

Animals were never officially considered deities themselves, but they were often believed to be the embodiment of a deity, a role the cat served for Bastet. The distinction was difficult for the public to grasp, and worship of cats became common. A bronze figure shows an Egyptian priest kneeling in worship before a very large cat wearing a great deal of gold jewellery. Archaeological explorations have unearthed numerous amulets of bronze, ivory, terracotta and lapis lazuli, made in the shape of a cat or bearing a picture of a cat.

The cult of Bastet and the concomitant worship of cats reached its height around 950 BC when Bastet began to take precedence over other Egyptian gods and goddesses. The main temple and centre of worship of Bastet was at the city of Bubastis on the Nile delta. The Greek historian Herodotus visited the temple of Bastet in Bubastis around 450 BC. He provides a vivid description of the temple and the annual festival held there. Bastet's temple is described as a magnificent red granite building, built in the form of a square. Walls carved with elaborate figures surrounded the sacred enclosure, a grove of huge trees, at the centre of which stood a statue of Bastet. Sacred cats lived inside the shrine and were ritually fed.

Little is known of the rituals of the temple, but Herodotus gives a detailed account of the annual festival, describing it as the most important and popular of the 'sacred assemblies'. Thousands of people evidently made a pilgrimage to Bubastis for the festival, often traveling by boat along the Nile. (As many as 700,000, according to Herodotus, who has long been suspected of occasionally exaggerating for effect.) Along the way, and on their arrival, the pilgrims celebrated with music, singing, dancing, sacrifice and consumption of large quantities of wine.

As a sacred animal, the death of a cat was serious business. When a household cat died, its Egyptian owners would shave their eyebrows in mourning and take the body to an embalmer for preservation. Entire graveyards devoted to cats have been found along the Nile, and elaborately wrapped, mummified cats show up regularly in tombs. Of course, cats weren't alone in being accorded this honour, but they do seem to have had a special place in the hearts of the people.

Egyptians took the connection of cats with the goddess so seriously that the murder of a cat was a capital offence. One Roman soldier who killed a cat was promptly lynched by the outraged locals. Their neighbours noticed the Egyptians' reverence for cats, and at least one group, the Persians, are believed to have taken advantage of it.

In 500 BC Persian soldiers laid siege to the Eyptian city of Pelusium, but the inhabitants of the city held out against the enemy, and the Persians were beginning to lose heart as they failed to achieve a final victory. They were on the verge of giving up the fight, when their leader Cambyses, son of Cyrus II the Great, seized on an idea. He sent his soldiers out to round up all the cats they could find. A few days later, the Persian forces made a final march on Pelusium, with each soldier carrying a cat. The Egyptians knew at once that they were defeated; they could not risk killing or even injuring any of the cats, so they quietly and immediately surrendered to the Persians without a single blow being exchanged. With the help of the drafted cats, the Persians went on to win further victories in Egypt.

The Cat with the Wooden Paw

WENDELL MARGRAVE
of Carbondale, Illinois, 1938

Jack Storme was the local cooper and blacksmith of Thebes in Illinois. He had a cat that stayed around the shop. The cat was the best mouser in the whole country, Jack said. He kept the shop free of rats and mice. But one day the cat got a forepaw cut off. After that he began to grow poor and thin and didn't take any interest in anything because he wasn't getting enough to eat.

So one day Jack decided to fix him up a wooden paw. He whittled one out with his knife and strapped it on the maimed leg. After that the cat began to grow sleek and fat again. Jack decided to stay at the shop one night to see how the cat managed it with his wooden paw.

After dark the cat got down in front of a mouse-hole and waited. Pretty soon a mouse peered out cautiously. Quick as a flash the cat seized it with his good paw and knocked it on the head with his wooden one. In no time that cat had eighteen mice piled up before the hole.

Stormy, the Long-Distance Cat

This amazing but true story began when Stormy, the rescue cat, suddenly disappeared from his new home in California. His owners – a mother and daughter – had moved from a farm in Minnesota three months earlier, and were heartbroken when Stormy went missing.

Astonishingly, Stormy was found nine months later, when his owners returned to Minnesota to visit relatives. Intuition prompted Stormy's human to check local Lost and Found ads, and a notice – "Found: All Grey Cat" – caught her attention. She went to check on the feline, and to her unbridled joy discovered that the cat was none other than Stormy! A veterinary surgeon confirmed Stormy's identity from the cat's dental records and the wayward cat was at last reunited with his delighted owners.

The amazing 2,000-mile journey had left Stormy a little worse for wear – he had lost 10 pounds in weight and his claws were worn right down, but he made a full recovery and has now decided to settle down in California.

The Undoing of Morning Glory Adolphus

N. MARGARET CAMPBELL

Morning Glory Adolphus is our oldest and most sedate cat. He has his own hunting preserves in a wooded ravine at the back of our house, and woe to the cat or dog who invades it. In his early youth he won an enviable reputation as a hunter of big game, and he had his own method of securing due recognition for his exploits. Whenever he captures a rabbit, a squirrel, a water-rat, or a snake, he hunts until he finds his mistress and lays the tribute proudly at her feet. This determination to be cited for bravery and prowess becomes a trifle embarrassing at times, especially when he drags a five-foot snake into the music-room and lets it wriggle on the rug to the horror and confusion of guests. But whatever the hazards, Adolphus is not to be thwarted of due publicity for his skill. If he were a man, he would be accompanied on all of his hunting-trips by a press-agent, and would have luncheon with the editors of all the sporting journals upon his return. As it is, without even a correspondence course in advertising, Adolphus manages quite well.

For the study of majestic dignity, tinged on occasions with lofty disdain, interpreters of muscular expression would do well to seek out Adolphus. He walks the highway without haste or concern for his personal survival in the midst of tooting automobiles and charging dogs. When a strange dog appears and mistakes Adolphus for an ordinary cat who may be chased for the sport of the thing, it is the custom of Adolphus to slow his pace somewhat and stretch out in the path of the oncoming enemy, assuming the pose and the expression of the sphinx. He is the graven image of repose and perfect muscular control. Only his slumbrous amber eyes burn unblinkingly, never leaving the enraged countenance of his enemy, who bears down upon him with exposed fangs and hackles erect. When the assault is too ferocious to be in good taste even among dogs, accompanied by hysterical yapping and snapping, Adolphus has been known to yawn in the face of his assailant, quite deliberately and very politely, as a gentleman of good breeding might when bored by an excessive display of emotion. Usually the dog mysteriously halts within a foot or so of those calm yellow eyes and describes a semi-circle within the range of those twin fires, filling the air with defiant taunts that gradually die away to foolish whimpering as he begins an undignified withdrawal, while Adolphus winks solemnly and stares past his cowering foe into a mysterious space undesecrated by blustering dogs.

A few dogs there have been who have failed to halt at the hypnotic command of those yellow eyes. Then there came a lightning-like flash of fur through the air, and Adolphus landed neatly on his victim's neck, his great claws beginning to rip with businesslike precision through the soft ears and forehead of the terrified dog. Perhaps the rumour of these encounters spread among the canine population of our neighbourhood, for it is never counted against the reputation of any dog as a fighter if he makes a wide detour of the regions frequented by Adolphus.

For years the rule of Adolphus among the cats of his own household had been undisputed. Then came Silver Paws, a handsome young rogue whose satiny coat was beautiful with broken silver and blue lights. There was no question about it, Silver Paws had a way with the ladies. While Adolphus still looked upon him as a frolicsome kitten whose sense of humour was unbalanced by a proper sense of dignity, he artfully won all hearts and easily became the centre of attraction wherever he appeared. It was plainly disgusting to Adolphus to see the way the conceited young thing arched his back expectantly whenever a human hand came near enough to caress him.

If Adolphus had had the small mind of a punster, he might have observed, after the cynical manner of others

who have lost their place in the public affections to an unworthy rival, that the glory was passing out of his name. But he was never one to surrender without a struggle. He went to his nightly hunt with cold murder in his heart and a high resolve to force the spotlight back upon himself. Daily he laid at the feet of his mistress older and wilder rabbits, fiercer-eyed rats, and longer snakes. All to no purpose. He even played the heroic role of the deliverer when his hated rival was treed by the grocer's dog. He simply walked calmly up to the tree where the dog was dancing wildly under the limb where the trembling Silver Paws clung, and the dog suddenly remembered that he really ought to catch up to the grocer's wagon and it wasn't much fun to bark at a silly kitten, anyway! When the frightened Silver Paws slid down the tree, Adolphus walked up to him with the self-righteous air of a benevolent gentleman who has rescued a lost soul not because the soul deserved it, but because he himself was made that way. This magnanimous act gave Adolphus a momentary advantage over his rival, but the fickle attentions of the household were soon centred upon the handsome young charmer again. Then Adolphus took to sitting about the house, gazing solemnly past the spot where Silver Paws was receiving the choicest bits of meat with many endearing words, and smoothing his whiskers with a reflective paw.

It was about this time that Silver Paws, to the consternation of the household, disappeared. A search was instituted in the neighbourhood, but he was gone without a trace, just as though he had been whisked away on a magic broom. Mournfully we gathered up the playthings he had left scattered over the house – a bit of fur on a string, a bright-coloured ball, some dried beans that rattled in the pod when batted about by a velvet paw – and of these remembrances we made a heap in his favourite rocking-chair. 'He'll want them if he ever comes back, we said.

A remarkable change had come over Morning Glory Adolphus. We had long honoured him as a crafty hunter and first-rate fighting-man, but we had judged him to be somewhat lacking in sentiment, a trifle indifferent and unresponsive, as was natural enough in one who had achieved no small amount of fame. What was our astonishment to find that he had become, overnight, warmly demonstrative in his affections and sympathetically desirous of turning our thoughts from useless brooding over the lost one. It was really touching to see the way he followed us about the house, sitting at our feet to sing with rapturous abandon wherever we happened to pause. Forgotten were the joys of the chase, the pleasant pastime of disciplining unmannerly dogs. For three whole days he gave himself up wholly to the business of love-making. If we attempted to ignore him, he threw himself at our feet and lay on his back at our mercy, as one who would say that he bared his faithful heart that we might kill him if we could not love him. He walked about the house with the proudly possessive air of a haughty ruler who has returned to his domains after an enforced absence, and he curled up blissfully on the cushions where his late rival had been accustomed to take his ease. Once we found him stretched contemptuously over the playthings that lay in a little heap in the rocking-chair. It must have been a bumpy sort of bed, but Adolphus looked happy and comfortable.

Suspicion instantly seized upon his mistress. 'Adolphus,' she said sternly, 'I believe you know what has become of our beautiful Silver Paws!' The accused rose stiffly to his full height, regarded her with the gravely innocent expression of an outraged deacon, and then, turning his back deliberately upon her, gave himself up again to the slumbers of the just.

But the suspicions of the household were not laid. 'Adolphus is trying too hard to be good,' they argued. 'It is not natural. There must be something on his conscience!' For this was Adolphus's way of raising a smoke-screen, as it were, to hide his evil deeds. They had observed this in the past. It was all very humiliating to a proud soul like Adolphus, and he showed his resentment by stalking out of the house and letting the screen-door slam behind him after the manner of any offended male.

The household followed him from afar. He walked straight to the ravine, where he was accustomed to hunt, and stood peering intently down into it over the edge of a cliff, his ears pricked forward, every line of him expressing gloating satisfaction, from his agitated whiskers to the tip of his quivering tail. It was hard to believe that he was the same kindly creature who had been making affectionate advances to us a few hours before. As we drew near we could hear a faint crying, pleading and pitiful, and down among the bushes we discovered our lost Silver Paws, too weak from loss of food to stand, and rather battered from the rough treatment he had received from his jailor.

The moment that Adolphus saw us looking into the ravine he withdrew in disgust, for he knew that his game was up. With lofty scorn he watched us gather up his banished rival, revive him with warm milk, caress and comfort him. With what dire threats had Adolphus kept his captive down in the ravine, within sound of our voices, all the long hours while he wooed us at his leisure, and what spell had he cast over him that the hungry kitten had not dared to come at our call?

While we rejoiced and scolded, the grocer's dog was observed coming around the corner of the house. He had grown bold during those days of weakness when Adolphus had been courting the ladies. But one look into the amber eyes of Adolphus, and he was off with a shriek, for he could see that the fighter was once more the master of his emotions.

U.S. Military 0, Cats 1

The United States Army once tried to train cats for use in military operations. Because cats have far more sensitive eyes than humans do, enabling them to see clearly even in near-total darkness, the Army thought they might be useful as guides for soldiers on night patrol. In 1968, a number of specially trained cats were shipped to Vietnam where they were to be tested in the jungle. The test, as most cat owners have probably already guessed, was a miserable failure.

The final official report contained the following comments: 'A squad, upon being ordered to move out, was led off in all different directions by the cats; on many occasions the animal led their troops racing through thick brush in pursuit of field mice and birds. ... Troops had to force the cats to follow the direction of the patrol; the practice often led to the animals stalking and attacking the dangling pack straps of the American soldiers marching directly in front of the animal. ... If the weather was inclement or even threatening inclemency, the cats were never anywhere to be found.'

A Vet's Life

JOHN BOWER

'Mrs Jones is on the telephone. Apparently her cat has just jumped off the sofa and its tail has dropped off!' My very able nurse had never delivered a more unusual or macabre message than that. At this stage I decided to speak to Mrs Jones myself as obviously there was some mistake – such a thing could not happen. It had! Mrs Jones's description of the furry object, about nine inches long, which was no longer part of Blackie the cat, left me in no doubt at all. I suggested she should bring both parts of Blackie in to my surgery where I hoped I could resolve the problem.

Blackie had indeed jumped off the sofa and lost his tail. About three weeks earlier, Blackie had been involved in a road accident from which he appeared to recover fairly rapidly. He had not regained the use of his tail, however, due to a `stretch fracture` at the base of the tail. This type of fracture is caused by a car tyre trapping the tail while a cat is still crossing the road at speed. This had, in this case, led to the death of the tail but not of Blackie. A minor cosmetic operation was needed to tidy up what was left of Blackie's tail and Blackie was as good as new – certainly a few inches better off than a Manx cat.

Cats do have problems with their tails. They seem to pay dearly for the extra bit of balance that the tail may give them. I always think of tail injuries as happening to cats that nearly got away with it. The tail, as I mentioned, is a fairly common site for a road accident injury. It is also often involved in injuries sustained in fights with other cats – presumably, either in cowardly cats which were running away at the time (too slowly), or possibly in cases in which the aggressor unfairly pounced from behind.

In the surgery, cats can be more difficult to handle and restrain than dogs. If a dog is a little fractious it is possible to muzzle it to prevent a bite and, of course, its claws are relatively harmless. A cat, however, can only be muzzled with extreme difficulty and usually distress is caused. The result is less co-operation than if it were not muzzled, and its claws can inflict most unpleasant wounds to the veterinary surgeon, the nurse or the owner. To reprimand a dog when necessary can help; in the case of cats it only makes the situation worse. Patience is the only real answer apart from a sedative when really necessary. Luckily for the profession, the attitude of the owner of an unco-operative cat is usually sympathetic to the veterinary surgeon. This varies from the mild, 'Do be careful, he may bite and scratch you', to the blunt, 'Don't trust him, he's a tiger.' This latter type of cat is usually brought in to the surgery trussed up in a small bag with perhaps his head protruding. One client of mine brings his cross-Siamese (very cross Siamese!) into the surgery from the waiting room by holding onto the scruff of the neck only. In this way the cat is brought in with all four legs and eighteen claws rigidly extended, teeth bared and a continuous, meaningful, warning growl coming from its mouth. I was horrified the first time this happened and tried to explain to the client that there were better ways of carrying his cat. However, a short abortive attempt to demonstrate other ways with his cat convinced me otherwise! I now see this cat only at his home, where he is considerably better behaved.

Some cats are great believers in the saying that attack is the best method of defence. The minute they are placed on the consulting table they make a determined attempt to climb up the person examining them. This is a highly effective method of avoiding an examination. Equally effective is the raised attacking forepaw when a hand comes anywhere near them. But once the cat is restrained by the scruff of the neck gently on the table, then it is usually possible to carry out a thorough examination.

A separate waiting room for cats away from their canine cousins is a sound idea in a veterinary practice, although this is not always possible owing to shortage of space. Certainly cats are more relaxed in such surroundings than sandwiched between a great dane and a wolfhound. It is always much safer to bring a cat to a surgery in a cat basket or zipper bag than just to carry it or wrap it in a towel. This minimizes any risk of escape which we all know can and does happen, and also ensures that the cat does not obtain such a close view of his neighbours in the waiting room.

I recall one escape with amusement now but great concern at the time that it happened. The surgery had finished and I was just contemplating a quiet evening when the door bell rang. At the time I lived above the surgery so there was no escape during off-duty hours. I answered the door and found a client holding her cat closely to her without even so much as a towel wrapped round it. The owner had misread the surgery hours and was presenting the cat for a routine check on a fractured leg which I had encased in a plaster cast the previous week. The poor cat took one look at me, realized immediately who I was and took off. The owner struggled to hold it but to no avail and within three seconds the cat had disappeared down the path, limping at lightning pace. I say limping because a quick look at the owner revealed that she was still holding the plaster cast! This was the one part of the cat that she had grasped when he struggled, to try to prevent him from escaping, but the Houdini had pulled his leg out of it and bolted! The story has a happy ending which is why I can now look back on it with amusement. Houdini limped straight home and was promptly returned to the surgery in a zipper bag. I applied a further plaster cast and within four weeks his leg was as good as new.

The most astonishing escapologist I ever handled was a ginger tom called Sandy. Sandy lived in a small coastal fishing village and, true to form on a Saturday evening, ate a piece of mackerel which unfortunately still contained the hook. This inevitably caught in Sandy's throat and my services were needed. This was no simple matter; the hook was anchored firmly in the throat and Sandy was in no way appreciative of my efforts to remove it. There was no alternative but to take him back to the surgery for a general anaesthetic in order to remove the hook. Sandy was popped into a strong wicker basket and placed in the back of my estate car. The sliding windows of the estate were closed. After a few miles, I decided to telephone the surgery to make sure there were no further urgent calls on the way back. Luckily there were not. On my arrival at the surgery, I lifted the basket out of the car and noticed that it was surprisingly light. Sandy had gone! The car, of course – he must be in the car! But I could feel myself beginning to panic. Mislaying a patient is not a common occurrence and I was hoping that this was a false alarm. It was not – Sandy was not in the car either. One sliding back window was now open. While I had stopped to make the telephone call, Sandy had escaped from an escape-proof basket (I have since decided that no wicker baskets are escape-proof!), opened one of the sliding windows and absconded. All of this at least ten miles from his home, on the wrong side of a very wide estuary, and with a fish hook in his mouth. I think it was at this stage that I nearly joined the Ministry – and not the Ministry of

Agriculture at that!

How was I to explain this to his devoted owners? I decided that there was no substitute for the truth, which I proceeded to tell them over the telephone. The news was received with unbelievable calm and equanimity, and apologies for not 'telling me that Sandy would open sliding doors, cupboards and windows'. I assured them that I would alert all the other veterinary practices, RSPCA and police. This I proceeded to do but, of course, none of them at this stage could help.

Three weeks later the RSPCA inspector arrived out of the blue with Sandy (dear, lovable Sandy) whom he had just picked up on the other side of the estuary from that on which he had been lost. I cannot explain to this day whether Sandy is a strong swimmer or had, in fact, jumped out of the moving car nearer to my surgery than I originally thought. Anyway, Sandy was back and looking fat and healthy at that but with the fish hook still firmly embedded in the back of his mouth. He had obviously managed to eat well despite the presence of the hook. I rapidly administered a general anaesthetic and removed the hook. Sandy was then returned to his surprisingly grateful owners and I exchanged all my wicker cat baskets for fibreglass ones.

I suppose this escapology is one aspect of intelligence in cats. It varies from cat to cat and my own three Siamese demonstrate quite dearly how the application of intelligence can vary. Guilia and Sadie are mother and daughter, and make up a very efficient door-opening team. They cannot open a door with a round knob but are experts at door handles. Sadie, being younger and fitter, jumps up at the handle and pulls it down with both forepaws as she falls to the ground, while Guilia, with precision timing, scrapes at the base of the door when the handle is depressed and opens it. They are so good at this that I have had to reverse the door handles of rooms which are forbidden to cats. The lounge falls into this category as the cats regard the lounge suite as their scratching posts. Rudyk, our third Siamese, has found an answer to this door provided we are in the lounge. He has noticed that, when the front door bell rings, we open the lounge door to go to answer it, which is when he nips in. He has also noticed that, in the bedroom upstairs, is an old-fashioned tassel pull to a bell which used to summon the maid in some past era, and that both bells sound alike. Amazingly, he has put two and two together and, when he wishes to come into the lounge, he runs upstairs, pulls the tassel, waits until one of us opens the lounge door to answer the front door and into the lounge he goes. We had not the heart to disconnect this bell.

Some of the more amusing incidents in the course of a working day are concerned with the sex of the cat and the problems arising if the owner is wrong about it. I see male cats called Sue and females called Jason but, luckily, a substantial proportion of Fluffys and Blackies, names which could apply to either sex. Owners can become quite indignant if told that the cat is not the sex that they thought it was. I recall a huge, obviously masculine, tabby with the typical male development of the cheeks and wide head, being presented at the surgery for the spay operation. I pointed out tactfully that spaying was the term applied to the female operation but that the male operation was called castration. To this the owner pointedly replied that she was aware of this and her cat was, of course, female. I rapidly checked that my original impression of the masculinity of the cat was biologically correct (which it was) and, feeling quite relieved, reassured the owner that the cat was indeed male. 'But it can't be,' replied the owner, 'it's called Tinkerbelle.'

The terms used for these routine operations are also great fun when modified by clients. Female cats are brought in to be splayed or sprayed; males to be incarcerated or castigated, while either sex can be brought in to the surgery to be neutralized or nurtured. One proud owner presented a superb little kitten and exclaimed, 'I want to know whether it is a boy or a girl and if it is a girl I want it incarcerated.' She was obviously terribly confused!

These operations are perfectly routine and side-effects are virtually nonexistent. In the case of dogs, bitches occasionally put on weight when spayed but only if fed too much of the wrong food. Cats, however, seem to regulate their body weight by correct feeding and exercise. Very few cats become highly overweight. An exception is a neuter male I am at present treating for a bladder complaint. He weighs 36lbs. When one considers that 10lbs is a fairly healthy weight for a normal male, this one is obviously grossly overweight. He somewhat resembles a miniature seal and is so wide that, when he sits lengthways along a wall, one front leg hangs down on each side of the wall. How he manages to climb the wall I have no idea! Apart from his present problem, which is not associated with his obesity, he remains active and healthy and loving with his owners. He does, however, resent my presence and interference for some reason and tries to make life difficult. Because of the amount of fat under his skin, he has no scruff, as this is obliterated by the fat. The scruff of the neck in cats was designed purely and simply for veterinary surgeons to hold on to while examining the cat and, when it is nonexistent, restraint of the cat becomes a major problem.

Some cats, however, appear to like and respect us. A colleague tells me of a blue-point Siamese cat called Buttons, brought to his surgery by his owners who live only a few doors away. Buttons had an injury to one ear, causing a large blood blister which had to be drained under an anaesthetic and then sutured to prevent its filling up again. The sutures are passed through the ear flap and knotted through a button to prevent the nylon suture pulling through the skin. Thereafter, Buttons used to arrive on his own at the surgery about every third day to have his buttons checked and finally removed. The only time his owners came with him was the first time.

The life we lead is sometimes exhausting but invariably rewarding. It is very satisfying to see patients recovering: to see Ginger running and climbing again after having sustained a broken leg in a road accident; to see Suki and kittens thriving after a Caesarean operation; to see Sandy recover from the slug-bait poisoning or even feline influenza. We do get attached to our patients but, as cats do not live to our life span, we necessarily see most of our patients pass on eventually over the years. It is very sad to see an old patient pass away when one can remember delivering him or her what seems like only yesterday. It is an interesting life, however, and the many bright moments brought about by such incidents as I have mentioned, either by the apparent wit of the cat or often the wit of the owner, send one home chuckling at the end of a hard day.

The Home Life of a Holy Cat

ARTHUR WIEGALL

One summer during a heat wave, when the temperature in the shade of my veranda in Luxor was 125° Fahrenheit, I went down to cooler Lower Egypt to pay a visit to an English friend of mine stationed at Zagazig, the native city which stands beside the ruins of ancient Bubastis.

He was about to leave Egypt and asked me whether I would like to have his cat, a dignified, mystical-minded, long-legged, small-headed, green-eyed female, whose orange-yellow hair, marked with greyish-black stripes in tabby pattern, was so short that she gave the impression of being naked – an impression, however, which did not in any way detract from her air of virginal chastity.

Her name was Basta, and though her more recent ancestors had lived wild amongst the ruins, she was so obviously a descendant of the holy cats of ancient times, who were incarnations of the goddess Basta, that I thought it only right to accept the offer and take her up to Luxor to live with me. To be the expert in charge of Egyptian antiquities and not have an ancient Egyptian cat to give an air of mystery to my headquarters had, indeed, always seemed to me to be somewhat wanting in showmanship on my part.

Thus it came about that, on my departure, I drove off to the railroad station with the usually dignified Basta bumping around and uttering unearthly howls inside a cardboard hat box, in the side of which I had cut a small round hole for ventilation. The people in the streets and on the station platform seemed to be under the impression that the noises were digestive and that I was in dire need of a doctor; and it was a great relief to my embarrassment when the hot and panting train steamed into Zagazig.

Fortunately, I found myself alone in the compartment, and the hatbox at my side had begun to cause me less anxiety, when suddenly Basta was seized with a sort of religious frenzy. The box rocked about, and presently out through the airhole came a long, snake-like paw which waved weirdly to and fro in space for a moment and then was withdrawn, its place being taken by a pink nose which pushed itself outward with such frantic force that the sides of the hole gave way, and out burst the entire sandy, sacred head.

She then began to choke, for the cardboard was pressing tightly around her neck; and to save her from strangulation I was obliged to tear the aperture open, whereupon she wriggled out, leaped in divine frenzy up the side of the carriage and prostrated herself on the network of the baggage-rack, where her hysteria caused her to lose all control of her internal arrangements and if I say modestly that she was overcome with nausea, I shall be telling but a part of the dreadful tale.

The rest of the journey was like a bad dream; but at the Cairo terminus, where I had to change into the night express for Luxor, I got the help of a native policeman who secured a large laundry basket from the sleeping-car department, and after a prolonged struggle, during which the train was shunted into a distant siding, we imprisoned the struggling Basta again.

The perspiring policeman and I then carried the basket at a run along the tracks back to the station in the sweltering heat of the late afternoon, and I just managed to catch my train; but during this second part of my journey Basta travelled in the baggage-van whence, in the hot and silent night, whenever we were at a standstill, her appalling incantations came drifting to my ears.

I opened the basket in an unfurnished spare room in my house, and like a flash Basta was up the bare wall and on to the curtain pole above the window. There she remained all day, in a sort of hypnotic trance; but at sunset the saucer of milk and plate of fish which I had provided for her at last enticed her down, and in the end she reconciled herself to her new surroundings and indicated by her behaviour that she was willing to accept my house as her earthly temple.

With Pedro, my pariah dog, there was not the slightest trouble; he had no strong feelings about cats, and she on her part graciously deigned to acknowledge his status – as, I believe, is generally the case in native households. She sometimes condescended to visit my horse and donkey in their stalls; and for Laura, my camel, she quickly developed a real regard, often sleeping for hours in her stable.

I was not worried as to how she would treat the chickens and pigeons, because her former owner at Zagazig had insisted upon her respecting his hen coop and pigeon cote; but I was a little anxious about the ducks, for she had not previously known any, and in ancient times her ancestors used to be trained to hunt wild geese and ducks and were fed with *pâté de foie gras*, or whatever it was called then, on holy days and anniversaries.

In a corner of the garden I had made a miniature duck pond which was sunk rather deeply in the ground and down to which I had cut a narrow, steeply sloping passage, or gangway. During the day, after the ducks had been up and down this slope several times, the surface used to become wet and slippery, and the ducks, having waddled down the first few inches, were forced to toboggan down the rest of it on their tails, with their two feet sticking out in front of them and their heads well up.

Basta was always fascinated by this slide and by the splash at the bottom, and used to sit and watch it all for hours, which made me think at first that she would one day spring at one of them; but she never did. Field mice, and water rats down by the Nile, were her only prey; and in connection with the former I may mention a curious occurrence.

One hot night I was sitting smoking my pipe on the veranda when my attention was attracted by two mice which had crept into the patch of brilliant moonlight before my feet and were boldly nibbling some crumbs left over from a cracker thrown to Pedro earlier in the evening. I watched them silently for a while and did not notice that Basta had seen them and was preparing to spring, nor did I observe a large white owl sitting aloft amongst the overhanging roses and also preparing to pounce.

Suddenly, and precisely at the same moment, the owl shot down on the mice from above and Basta leaped at them from beside me. There was a collision and a wild scuffle; fur and feathers flew; I fell out of my chair; and then the owl made off screeching in one direction and the cat dashed away in the other; while the mice, practically clinging to each other, remained for a moment or so too terrified to move.

During the early days of her residence in Luxor, Basta often used to go down to the edge of the Nile to fish with her paw; but she never caught anything, and in the end she got a fright and gave it up. I was sitting by the river watching her trying to catch one of a little shoal of small fish which were sunning themselves in the shallow water when there came swimming into view a twelve or fourteen-inch fish which I recognized (by its whiskers and the absence of a dorsal fin) as the electric cat fish, pretty common in the Nile – a strange creature able to give you an electric shock like hitting your funny bone.

These fish obtain their food in a curious way: they hang round any shoal of small fry engaged in feeding, and then glide quietly into their midst and throw out this electric shock, whereupon the little fellows are all sick to the stomach, and the big fellow gets their disgorged dinners.

I was just waiting to see this happen with my own eyes – for it had always seemed a bit far-fetched – when Basta made a dart at the intruder with her paw and got a shock. She uttered a yowl as though somebody had trodden on her and leaped high in the air; and never again did she put her foot near the water. She was content after that with our daily offering of a fish brought from the market and fried for her like a burnt sacrifice.

Basta had a most unearthly voice, and when she was feeling emotional would let out a wail which at first was like the crying of a phantom baby and then became the tuneless song of a lunatic, and finally developed into the blood-curdling howl of a soul in torment. And when she spat, the percussion was like that of a spring-gun.

There were some wild cats or, rather, domestic cats who, like Basta's own forebears, had taken to a wild life, living in a grove of trees beside the river just beyond my garden wall; and it was generally the proximity of one of these which started her off; but sometimes the outburst was caused by her own unfathomable thoughts as she went her mysterious ways in the darkness of the night.

I think she must have been clairvoyant, for she often seemed to be seeing things not visible to me. Sometimes, perhaps when she was cleaning fish or mouse from her face, she would pause with one foot off the ground and stare in front of her, and then back away with bristling hair or go forward with friendly little mewing noises; and sometimes she would leap off a chair or sofa, her tail lashing and her green eyes dilated. But it may have been worms.

Once I saw her standing absolutely rigid and tense on the lawn, staring at the rising moon; and then all of a sudden she did a sort of dance such as cats sometimes do when they are playing with other cats. But there was no other cat and, any way, Basta never played; she never forgot that she was a holy cat.

Her chaste hauteur was so great that she would not move out of the way when people were walking about, and many a time her demoniacal shriek and perhaps a crash of breaking glass informed the household that somebody had tripped over her. It was astonishing, however, how quickly she recovered her dignity and how well she maintained the pretence that whatever happened to her was at her own celestial wish and was not our doing.

If I called her she would pretend not to hear, but would come a few moments later when it could appear that she had thought of doing so first; and if I lifted her off a chair she would jump back on to it and then descend with dignity as though of her own free will. But in this, of course, she was more like a woman than like a divinity.

The Egyptian cat is a domesticated species of the African wild-cat, and no doubt its strange behaviour and its weird voice were the cause of it being regarded as sacred in ancient times; but, although the old gods and their worship have been forgotten these many centuries, the traditional sanctity of the race has survived.

Modern Egyptians think it unlucky to hurt a cat and, in the native quarters of Cairo and other cities, hundreds of cats are daily fed at the expense of benevolent citizens. They say that they do this because cats are so useful to mankind in killing off mice and other pests; but actually it is an unrecognized survival of the old beliefs.

In the days of the Pharaohs, when a cat died the men of the household shaved off their eyebrows and sat around wailing and rocking themselves to and fro in simulated anguish. The body was embalmed and buried with solemn rites in the local cats' cemetery, or was sent down to Bubastis to rest in the shadow of the temple of their patron goddess. I myself have dug up hundreds of mummified cats; and once, when I had a couple of dozen of the best specimens standing on my veranda waiting to be dispatched to the Cairo Museum, Basta was most excited about it, and walked around sniffing at them all day. They certainly smelled awful.

On my lawn there was a square slab of stone which had once been the top of an altar dedicated to the sun god, but was now used as a sort of low garden table; and sometimes when she had caught a mouse she used to deposit the chewed corpse upon this slab – nobody could think why, unless, as I always told people, she was really making an offering to the sun. It was most mysterious of her; but it led once to a very unfortunate episode.

A famous French antiquarian, who was paying a polite call, was sitting with me beside this sacred stone, drinking afternoon tea and eating fresh dates, when Basta appeared on the scene with a small dead mouse in her mouth, which in her usual way she deposited upon the slab – only on this occasion she laid it on my guest's plate, which was standing on the slab.

We were talking at the moment and did not see her do this and, anyhow, the Frenchman was as blind as a bat; and, of course, as luck would have it, he immediately picked up the wet, mole-coloured mouse instead of a ripe brown date, and the thing had almost gone into his mouth before he saw what it was and, with a yell, flung it into the air.

It fell into his upturned sun helmet which was lying on the grass beside him; but he did not see where it had gone and, jumping angrily to his feet in the momentary belief that I had played a schoolboy joke on him, he snatched up his helmet and was in the act of putting it on his head when the mouse tumbled out on to the front of his shirt and slipped down inside his buttoned jacket.

At this he went more or less mad, danced about, shook himself, and finally trod on Basta, who completed his frenzy by uttering a fiendish howl and digging her claws into his leg. The dead mouse, I am glad to say, fell on to the grass during the dance without passing through his roomy trousers, as I had feared it might; and Basta, recovering her dignity, picked it up and walked off with it.

It is a remarkable fact that, during the five or six years she spent with me, she showed no desire to be anything but a spinster all her life, and when I arranged a marriage for her she displayed such dignified but violent antipathy towards the bridegroom that the match was a failure. In the end, however, she fell in love with one of the wild cats who lived among the trees beyond my wall, and nothing could prevent her going off to visit him from time to time, generally at dead of night.

He did not care a hoot about her sanctity, and she was feminine enough to enjoy the novelty of being roughly treated. I never actually saw him, for he did not venture into the garden, but I used to hear him knocking her about outside my gates; and when she came home, scratched and bitten and muttering something about holy cats, it was plain that she was desperately happy. She licked her wounds, indeed, with deep and voluptuous satisfaction.

A dreadful change came over her. She lost her precious dignity and was restless and inclined to be savage; her digestion played embarrassing tricks on her; and once she mortally offended Laura by clawing her nose. There was a new glint in her green eyes as she watched the ducks sliding into the pond; the pigeons interested her for the first time; and for the first time, too, she ate the mice she caught.

Then she began to disappear for a whole day or night at a time, and once when I went in search of her amongst the trees outside and found her sharpening her claws on a branch above my head, she put her ears back and hissed at me until I could see every one of her teeth and halfway down her pink throat. I tried by every method to keep her at home when she came back, but it was all in vain, and at last she left me forever.

Weeks afterwards I caught sight of her once again amongst the trees, and it was evident that she was soon to become a mother. She gave me a friendly little mew this time, but she would not let me touch her; and presently she slipped away into the undergrowth. I never knew what became of her.

The White and Black Dynasties

THÉOPHILE GAUTIER

A cat brought from Havana by Mademoiselle Anïta de la Penuela, a young Spanish artist whose studies of white angoras may still be seen gracing the printsellers' windows, produced the daintiest little kitten imaginable. It was just like a swan's-down powder-puff, and on account of its immaculate whiteness it received the name of Pierrot. When it grew big this was lengthened to Don Pierrot de Navarre as being more grandiose and majestic.

Don Pierrot, like all animals which are spoilt and made much of, developed a charming amiability of character. He shared the life of the household with all the pleasure which cats find in the intimacy of the domestic hearth. Seated in his usual place near the fire, he really appeared to understand what was being said, and to take an interest in it.

His eyes followed the speakers, and from time to time he would utter little sounds, as though he too wanted to make remarks and give his opinion on literature, which was our usual topic of conversation. He was very fond of books, and when he found one open on a table he would lie on it, look at the page attentively, and turn over the leaves with his paw; then he would end by going to sleep, for all the world as if he were reading a fashionable novel.

Directly I took up a pen he would jump on my writing-desk and with deep attention watch the steel nib tracing black spider-legs on the expanse of white paper, and his head would turn each time I began a new line. Sometimes he tried to take part in the work, and would attempt to pull the pen out of my hand, no doubt in order to write himself, for he was an aesthetic cat, like Hoffman's Murr, and I strongly suspect him of having scribbled his memoirs at night on some house-top by the light of his phosphorescent eyes. Unfortunately these lucubrations have been lost.

Don Pierrot never went to bed until I came in. He waited for me inside the door, and as I entered the hall he would rub himself against my legs and arch his back, purring joyfully all the time. Then he proceeded to walk in front of me like a page, and if I had asked him, he would certainly have carried the candle for me. In this fashion he escorted me to my room and waited while I undressed; then he would jump on the bed, put his paws round my neck, rub noses with me, and lick me with his rasping little pink tongue, while giving vent to soft inarticulate cries, which clearly expressed how pleased he was to see me again. Then when his transports of affection had subsided, and the hour for repose had come, he would balance himself on the rail of the bedstead and sleep there like a bird perched on a bough. When I woke in the morning he would come and lie near me until it was time to get up. Twelve o'clock was the hour at which I was supposed to come in. On this subject Pierrot had all the notions of a concierge.

At that time we had instituted little evening gatherings among a few friends, and had formed a small society, which we called the Four Candles Club, the room in which we met being, as it happened, lit by four candles in silver candlesticks, which were placed at the corners of the table.

Sometimes the conversation became so lively that I forgot the time, at the risk of finding, like Cinderella, my carriage turned into a pumpkin and my coachman into a rat.

Pierrot waited for me several times until two o'clock in the morning, but in the end my conduct displeased him, and he went to bed without me. This mute protest against my innocent dissipation touched me so much that ever after I came home regularly at midnight. But it was a long time before Pierrot forgave me. He wanted to be sure that it was not a sham repentance; but when he was convinced of the sincerity of my conversion, he deigned to take me into favour again, and he resumed his nightly post in the entrance-hall.

To gain the friendship of a cat is not an easy thing. It is a philosophic, well-regulated, tranquil animal, a creature of habit and a lover of order and cleanliness. It does not give its affections indiscriminately. It will consent to be your friend if you are worthy of the honour, but it will not be your slave. With all its affection, it preserves its freedom of judgement, and it will not do anything for you which it considers unreasonable; but once it has given its love, what absolute confidence, what fidelity of affection! It will make itself the companion of your hours of work, of loneliness, or of sadness. It will lie the whole evening on your knee, purring and happy in your society, and leaving the company of creatures of its own kind to be with you. In vain the sound of caterwauling reverberates from the house-tops, inviting it to one of those cats' evening parties where essence of red-herring takes the place of tea. It will not be tempted, but continues to keep its vigil with you. If you put it down it climbs up again quickly, with a sort of crooning noise, which is like a gentle reproach. Sometimes, when seated

in front of you, it gazes at you with such soft, melting eyes, such a human and caressing look, that you are almost awed, for it seems impossible that reason can be absent from it.

Don Pierrot had a companion of the same race as himself, and no less white. All the imaginable snowy comparisons it were possible to pile up would not suffice to give an idea of that immaculate fur, which would have made ermine look yellow.

I called her Seraphita, in memory of Balzac's Swedenborgian romance. The heroine of that wonderful story, when she climbed the snow peaks of the Falberg with Minna, never shone with a more pure white radiance. Seraphita had a dreamy and pensive character. She would lie motionless on a cushion for hours, not asleep, but with eyes fixed in rapt attention on scenes invisible to ordinary mortals.

Caresses were agreeable to her, but she responded to them with great reserve, and only to those of people whom she favoured with her esteem, which it was not easy to gain. She liked luxury, and it was always in the newest armchair or on the piece of furniture best calculated to show off her swan-like beauty, that she was to be found. Her toilette took an immense time. She would carefully smooth her entire coat every morning, and wash her face with her paw, and every hair on her body shone like new silver when brushed by her pink tongue. If anyone touched her she would immediately efface all traces of the contact, for she could not endure being ruffled. Her elegance and distinction gave one an idea of aristocratic birth, and among her own kind she must have been at least a duchess. She had a passion for scents. She would plunge her nose into bouquets, and nibble a perfumed handkerchief with little paroxysms of delight. She would walk about on the dressing-table sniffling the stoppers of the scent-bottles, and she would have loved to use the violet powder if she had been allowed. Such was Seraphita, and never was a cat more worthy of a poetic name.

Don Pierrot de Navarre, being a native of Havana, needed a hot-house temperature. This he found indoors, but the house was surrounded by large gardens, divided up by palings through which a cat could easily slip, and planted with big trees in which hosts of birds twittered and sang; and sometimes Pierrot, taking advantage of an open door, would go out hunting of an evening and run over the dewy grass and flowers. He would then have to wait till morning to be let in again, for although he might come mewing under the windows, his appeal did not always wake the sleepers inside.

He had a delicate chest, and one colder night than usual he took a chill which soon developed into consumption. Poor Pierrot, after a year of coughing, became wasted and thin, and his coat, which formerly boasted such a snowy gloss, now put one in mind of the lustreless white of a shroud. His great limpid eyes looked enormous in his attenuated face. His pink nose had grown pale, and he would walk sadly along the sunny wall with slow steps, and watch the yellow autumn leaves whirling up in spirals. He looked as though he were reciting Millevoye's elegy. There is nothing more touching than a sick animal; it submits to suffering with such gentle, pathetic resignation.

Everything possible was done to try and save Pierrot. He had a very clever doctor who sounded him and felt his pulse. He ordered him asses' milk, which the poor creature drank willingly enough out of his little china saucer. He lay for hours on my knee like the ghost of a sphinx, and I could feel the bones of his spine like the beads of a rosary under my fingers. He tried to respond to my caresses with a feeble purr which was like a death rattle.

When he was dying he lay panting on his side, but with a supreme effort he raised himself and came to me with dilated eyes in which there was a look of intense supplication. This look seemed to say: 'Cannot you save me, you who are a man?' Then he staggered a short way with eyes already glazing, and fell down with such a lamentable cry, so full of despair and anguish, that I was pierced with silent horror. He was buried at the bottom of the garden under a white rosebush which still marks his grave.

Seraphita died two or three years later of diphtheria, against which no science could prevail. She rests not far from Pierrot. With her the white dynasty became extinct, but not the family. To this snow-white pair were born three kittens as black as ink. Let him explain this mystery who can.

Just at that time Victor Hugo's *Misérables* was in great vogue, and the names of the characters in the novel were on everyone's lips. I called the two male kittens Enjolras and Gavroche, while the little female received the name of Eponine.

They were perfectly charming in their youth. I trained them like dogs to fetch and carry a bit of paper crumpled into a ball, which I threw for them. In time they learnt to fetch it from the tops of cupboards, from behind chests or from the bottom of tall vases, out of which they would pull it very cleverly with their paws. When they grew up they disdained such frivolous games, and acquired that calm philosophic temperament which is the true nature of cats.

To people landing in America in a slave colony all negroes are negroes, and indistinguishable from one another. In the same way, to careless eyes, three black cats are three black cats; but attentive observers make no such mistake. Animal physiognomy varies as much as that of men, and I could distinguish perfectly between those faces, all three as black as Harlequin's mask, and illuminated by emerald disks shot with gold.

Enjolras was by far the handsomest of the three. He

was remarkable for his great leonine head and big ruff, his powerful shoulders, long back and splendid feathery tail. There was something theatrical about him, and he seemed to be always posing like a popular actor who knows he is being admired. His movements were slow, undulating and majestic. He put each foot down with as much circumspection as if he were walking on a table covered with Chinese bric-à-brac or Venetian glass. As to his character, he was by no means a stoic, and he showed a love of eating which that virtuous and sober young man, his namesake, would certainly have disapproved. Enjolras would undoubtedly have said to him like the angel to Swedenborg: 'You eat too much.'

I humoured this gluttony, which was as amusing as a gastronomic monkey's, and Enjolras attained a size and weight seldom reached by the domestic cat. It occurred to me to have him shaved poodle-fashion, so as to give the finishing touch to his resemblance to a lion.

We left him his mane and a big tuft at the end of his tail, and I would not swear that we did not give him mutton-chop whiskers on his haunches like those Munito wore. Thus tricked out, it must be confessed he was much more like a Japanese monster than an African lion. Never was a more fantastic whim carved out of a living animal. His shaven skin took odd blue tints, which contrasted strangely with his black mane.

Gavroche, as though desirous of calling to mind his namesake in the novel, was a cat with an arch and crafty expression of countenance. He was smaller than Enjolras, and his movements were comically quick and brusque. In him absurd capers and ludicrous postures took the place of the banter and slang of the Parisian gamin. It must be confessed that Gavroche had vulgar tastes. He seized every possible occasion to leave the drawing-room in order to go and make up parties in the backyard, or even in the street, with stray cats,

'*De naissance quelconque et de sang peu prouvé,*'

in which doubtful company he completely forgot his dignity as cat of Havana, son of Don Pierrot de Navarre, grandee of Spain of the first order, and of the aristocratic and haughty Doña Seraphita.

Sometimes in his truant wanderings he picked up emaciated comrades, lean with hunger, and brought them to his plate of food to give them a treat in his good-natured, lordly way. The poor creatures, with ears laid back and watchful side-glances, in fear of being interrupted in their free meal by the broom of the housemaid, swallowed double, triple, and quadruple mouthfuls, and, like the famous dog Siete-Aguas (seven waters) of Spanish posadas (inns), they licked the plate as clean as if it had been washed and polished by one of Gerard Dow's or Mieris's Dutch housewives.

Seeing Gavroche's friends reminded me of a phrase which illustrates one of Gavarni's drawings, *'Ils sont jolis les amis dont vous êtes susceptible d'aller avec!'* ('Pretty kind of friends you like to associate with!')

But that only proved what a good heart Gavroche had, for he could easily have eaten all the food himself.

The cat named after the interesting Eponine was more delicate and slender than her brothers. Her nose was rather long, and her eyes slightly oblique, and green as those of Pallas Athene. Her nose was of velvety black, with the grain of a fine Périgord truffle; her whiskers were in a perpetual state of agitation, all of which gave her a peculiarly expressive countenance. Her superb black coat was always in motion, and was watered and shot with shadowy markings. Never was there a more sensitive, nervous, electric animal. If one stroked her two or three times in the dark, blue sparks would fly crackling out of her fur.

Eponine attached herself particularly to me, like the Eponine of the novel to Marius, but I, being less taken up with Cosette than that handsome young man, could accept the affection of this gentle and devoted cat, who still shares the pleasures of my suburban retreat and is the inseparable companion of my hours of work.

She comes running up when she hears the front-door bell, receives the visitors, conducts them to the drawing-room, talks to them – yes, talks to them – with little chirruping sounds, that do not in the least resemble the language cats use in talking to their own kind, but which simulate the articulate speech of man. What does she say? She says in the clearest way, 'Will you be good enough to wait till monsieur comes down? Please look at the pictures, or chat with me in the meantime, if that will amuse you.' Then when I come in she discreetly retires to an armchair or a corner of the piano, like a well-bred animal who knows what is correct in good society. Pretty little Eponine gave so many proofs of intelligence, good disposition and sociability, that by common consent she was raised to the dignity of a person, for it was quite evident that she was possessed of higher reasoning power than mere instinct. This dignity conferred on her the privilege of eating at table like a person instead of out of a saucer in a corner of the room like an animal.

So Eponine had a chair next to me at breakfast and dinner, but on account of her small size she was allowed to rest her two front paws on the edge of the table. Her place was laid, without spoon or fork, but she had her glass. She went right through dinner dish by dish, from soup to dessert, waiting for her turn to be helped, and behaving with such propriety and nice manners as one would like to see in many children. She made her appearance at the first sound of the bell, and on going into the dining-room one found her already in her place, sitting up in her chair with her paws resting on the edge of the tablecloth, and seeming to offer you her little face to kiss, like a well-brought-up little girl who is affectionately polite towards her parents and elders.

As one finds flaws in diamonds, spots on the sun, and shadows on perfection itself, so Eponine, it must be confessed, had a passion for fish. She shared this in common with all other cats. Contrary to the Latin proverb,

'Catus amat pieces, sed non vult tingere plantas,'

she would willingly have dipped her paw into the water if by so doing she could have pulled out a trout or a young carp. She became nearly frantic over fish, and, like a child who is filled with the expectation of dessert, she sometimes rebelled at her soup when she knew (from previous investigations in the kitchen) that fish was coming. When this happened she was not helped, and I would say to her coldly: 'Mademoiselle, a person who is not hungry for soup cannot be hungry for fish,' and the dish would be pitilessly carried away from under her nose. Convinced that matters were serious, greedy Eponine would swallow her soup in all haste, down to the last drop, polishing off the last crumb of bread or bit of macaroni, and would then turn round and look at me with pride, like someone who has conscientiously done his duty. She was then given her portion, which she consumed with great satisfaction, and after tasting of every dish in turn, she would finish up by drinking a third of a glass of water.

When I am expecting friends to dinner Eponine knows there is going to be a party before she sees the guests. She looks at her place, and if she sees a knife and fork by her plate she decamps at once and seats herself on a music-stool, which is her refuge on these occasions.

Let those who deny reasoning powers to animals explain if they can this little fact, apparently so simple, but which contains a whole series of inductions. From the presence near her plate of those implements which man alone can use, this observant and reflective cat concludes that she will have to give up her place for that day to a guest, and promptly proceeds to do so. She never makes a mistake; but when she knows the visitor well she climbs on his knee and tries to coax a tit-bit out of him by her pretty caressing ways.

Min and the Mouse

HENRY DAVID THOREAU

Min caught a mouse, and was playing with it in the yard. It had got away from her once or twice and she had caught it again, and now it was stealing off again, as she was complacently watching it with her paws tucked under her, when her friend, Riorden, a stout cock, stepped up inquisitively, looked down at the mouse with one eye, turning its head, then picked it up by the tail, gave it two or three whacks on the ground, and giving it a dexterous toss in the air, caught the mouse in its open mouth. It went, head foremost and alive, down Riorden's capacious throat in the twinkling of an eye, never again to be seen in this world; Min all the while, with paws comfortably tucked under her, looking on unconcerned. What did one mouse matter, more or less, to her? The cock walked off amid the currant-bushes, stretched his neck up and gulped once or twice, and the deed was accomplished. Then he crowed lustily in celebration of the exploit. It might be set down among the *Gesta Gallorum*. There were several human witnesses. It is a question whether Min ever understood where that mouse went to. She sits composedly sentinel, with paws tucked under her, a good part of her days at present, by some ridiculous little hole, [awaiting] the possible entry of a mouse.

Discipline

AGNES REPPLIER

This extract from *The Fireside Sphinx* was written in 1901 by the American essayist.

A female cat is kept young in spirit and supple in body by the restless vivacity of her kittens. She plays with her little ones, fondles them, pursues them if they roam too far, and corrects them sharply for all the faults to which feline infancy is heir. A kitten dislikes being washed quite as much as a child does, especially in the neighbourhood of its ears. It tries to escape the infliction, rolls away, paddles with its little paws, and behaves as naughtily as it knows how, until a smart slap brings it suddenly back to subjection. Pussy has no confidence in moral suasion, but implicitly follows Solomon's somewhat neglected advice.

I was once told a pleasant story of an English cat who had reared several large families, and who, dozing one day before the nursery fire, was disturbed and annoyed by the whining of a fretful child. She bore it as long as she could, waiting for the nurse to interpose her authority; then, finding passive endurance had outstripped the limits of her patience, she arose, crossed the room, jumped on the sofa, and twice with her strong soft paw, which had chastised many an erring kitten, deliberately boxed the little girl's ears – after which she returned to her slumbers.

211

Midshipman, the Cat

JOHN COLEMAN ADAMS

This is a true story about a real cat who, for aught I know, is still alive and following the sea for a living. I hope to be excused if I use the pronouns 'who' and 'he' instead of 'which' and 'it,' in speaking of this particular cat; because although I know very well that the grammars all tell us that 'he' and 'who' apply to persons, while 'it' and 'which' apply to things, yet this cat of mine always seemed to us who knew him to be so much like a human being that I find it unsatisfactory to speak of him in any other way. There are some animals of whom you prefer to say 'he,' just as there are persons whom you sometimes feel like calling 'it.'

The way we met this cat was after this fashion: It was back somewhere in the seventies, and a party of us were cruising east from Boston in the little schooner-yacht *Eyvor*. We had dropped into Marblehead for a day and a night, and some of the boys had gone ashore in the tender. As they landed on the wharf, they found a group of small boys running sticks into a woodpile, evidently on a hunt for something inside.

'What have you in there?' asked one of the yachtsmen.

'Nothin' but a cat,' said the boys.

'Well, what are you doing to him?'

'Oh, pokin' him up! When he comes out we'll rock

him,' was the answer, in good Marblehead dialect.

'Well, don't do it any more. What's the use of tormenting a poor cat? Why don't you take somebody of your size?'

The boys slowly moved off, a little ashamed and a little afraid of the big yachtsman who spoke; and when they were well out of sight the yachtsmen went on, too, and thought no more about the cat they had befriended. But when they had wandered about the tangled streets of the town for a little while, and paid the visits which all good yachtsmen pay, to the grocery and the post office and the apothecary's soda fountain, they returned to the wharf and found their boat. And behold, there in the stern sheets sat the little gray-and-white cat of the woodpile! He had crawled out of his retreat and made straight for the boat of his champions. He seemed in no wise disturbed or disposed to move when they jumped on board, nor did he show anything but pleasure when they stroked and patted him. But when one of the boys started to put him ashore, the plucky little fellow showed his claws; and no sooner was he set on his feet at the edge of the wharf than he turned about and jumped straight back into the boat.

'He wants to go yachting,' said one of the party, whom we called 'the Bos'n.'

'Ye might as wal take the cat,' said a grizzly old fisherman standing on the wharf. 'He doesn't belong to anybody, and ef he stays here the boys'll worry him t'death.'

'Let's take him aboard,' said the yachtsmen. 'It's good luck to have a cat on board ship.'

Whether it was good luck to the ship or not, it was very clear that pussy saw it meant good luck to him, and curled himself down in the bottom of the boat, with a look that meant business. Evidently he had thought the matter all over and made up his mind that this was the sort of people he wanted to live with; and, being a

Marblehead cat, it made no difference to him whether they lived afloat or ashore; he was going where they went, whether they wanted him or not. He had heard the conversation from his place in the woodpile, and had decided to show his gratitude by going to sea with these protectors of his. By casting in his lot with theirs he was paying them the highest compliment of which a cat is capable. It would have been the height of impoliteness not to recognize his distinguished appreciation. So he was allowed to remain in the boat, and was taken off to the yacht.

Upon his arrival there, a council was held, and it was unanimously decided that the cat should be received as a member of the crew; and as we were a company of amateur sailors, sailing our own boat, each man having his particular duties, it was decided that the cat should be appointed midshipman, and should be named after his position. So he was at once and ever after known as 'Middy.' Everybody took a great interest in him, and he took an impartial interest in everybody – though there were two people on board to whom he made himself particularly agreeable. One was the quiet, kindly professor, the captain of the *Eyvor*; the other was Charlie, our cook and only hired hand. Middy, you see, had a seaman's true instinct as to the official persons with whom it was his interest to stand well.

It was surprising to see how quickly Middy made himself at home. He acted as if he had always been at sea. He was never seasick, no matter how rough it was or how uncomfortable any of the rest of us were. He roamed wherever he wanted to, all over the boat. At mealtimes he came to the table with the rest, sat up on a valise, and lapped his milk and took what bits of food were given him, as if he had eaten that way all his life. When the sails were hoisted it was his especial joke to jump upon the main gaff and be hoisted with it; and once he stayed on his perch till the sail was at the masthead.

One of us had to go aloft and bring him down. When we had come to anchor and everything was snug for the night, he would come on deck and scamper out on the main boom, and race from there to the bowsprit end as fast as he could gallop, then climb, monkey-fashion, halfway up the masts, and drop back to the deck or dive down into the cabin and run riot among the berths.

One day, as we were jogging along, under a pleasant southwest wind, and everybody was lounging and dozing after dinner, we heard the Bos'n call out, 'Stop that, you fellows!' and a moment after, 'I tell you, quit! Or I'll come up and make you!'

We opened our lazy eyes to see what was the matter, and there sat the Bos'n, down in the cabin, close to the companionway, the tassel of his knitted cap coming nearly up to the combings of the hatch; and on the deck outside sat Middy, digging his claws into the tempting yarn, and occasionally going deep enough to scratch the Bos'n's scalp.

When night came and we were all settled down in bed, it was Middy's almost invariable custom to go the rounds of all the berths, to see if we were properly tucked in, and to end his inspection by jumping into the captain's bed, treading himself a comfortable nest there among the blankets, and curling himself down to sleep. It was his own idea to select the captain's berth as the only proper place in which to turn in.

But the most interesting trait in Middy's character did not appear until he had been a week or so on board. Then he gave us a surprise. It was when we were lying in Camden Harbor. Everybody was going ashore to take a tramp among the hills, and Charlie, the cook, was coming too, to row the boat back to the yacht.

Middy discovered that he was somehow 'getting left.' Being a prompt and very decided cat, it did not take him long to make up his mind what to do. He ran to the low rail of the yacht, put his forepaws on it, and gave us a long, anxious look. Then as the boat was shoved off he raised his voice in a plaintive mew. We waved him a good-bye, chaffed him pleasantly, and told him to mind the anchor, and have dinner ready when we got back.

That was too much for his temper. As quick as a flash he had dived overboard, and was swimming like a water spaniel, after the dinghy!

That was the strangest thing we had ever seen in all our lives! We were quite used to elephants that could play at seesaw, and horses that could fire cannon, to learned pigs and to educated dogs; but a cat that of his own accord would take to the water like a full-blooded Newfoundland was a little beyond anything we had ever heard of. Of course the boat was stopped, and Middy was taken aboard drenched and shivering, but perfectly happy to be once more with the crew. He had been ignored and slighted; but he had insisted on his rights, and as soon as they were recognized he was quite contented.

Of course, after that we were quite prepared for anything that Middy might do. And yet he always managed to surprise us by his bold and independent behaviour. Perhaps his most brilliant performance was a visit he paid a few days after his swim in Camden Harbor.

We were lying becalmed in a lull of the wind off the entrance to Southwest Harbor. Near us, perhaps a cable's-length away, lay another small yacht, a schooner hailing from Lynn. As we drifted along on the tide, we noticed that Middy was growing very restless; and presently we found him running along the rail and looking eagerly toward the other yacht. What did he see – or smell – over there which interested him? It could not be the dinner, for they were not then cooking. Did he recognize any of his old chums from Marblehead? Perhaps there were some cat friends of his on the other craft. Ah, that was it! There they were on the deck, playing and frisking together – two kittens! Middy had spied them, and was longing to take a nearer look. He ran up and down the deck, mewing and snuffing the air. He stood up in his favourite position when on lookout, with his forepaws on the rail. Then, before we realized what he was doing, he had plunged overboard again, and was making for the other boat as fast as he could swim! He had attracted the attention of her company, and no sooner did he come up alongside than they prepared to welcome him. A fender was lowered, and when Middy saw it he swam toward it, caught it with his forepaws, clambered along it to the gunwale, and in a twinkling was over the side and on the deck scraping acquaintance with the strange kittens.

How they received him I hardly know, for by that time our boat was alongside to claim the runaway. And we were quite of the mind of the skipper of the *Winnie L.*, who said, as he handed our bold midshipman over the side, 'Well, that beats all *my* going a-fishing!'

Only a day or two later Middy was very disobedient when we were washing decks one morning. He trotted about in the wet till his feet were drenched, and then retired to dry them on the white spreads of the berths below. That was quite too much for the captain's patience. Middy was summoned aft, and, after a sound rating, was hustled into the dinghy which was moored astern, and shoved off to the full length of her painter. The punishment was a severe one for Middy, who could bear anything better than exile from his beloved shipmates. So of course he began to exercise his ingenious little brain to see how he could escape. Well under the overhang of the yacht he spied, just about four inches out of water, a little shoulder of the rudder. That was enough for him. He did not stop to think whether he would be any better off there. It was a part of the yacht, and that was home. So overboard he went, swam for the rudder, scrambled on to it, and began howling piteously to be taken on deck again; and, being a spoiled and much-indulged cat, he was soon rescued from his uncomfortable roosting place and restored to favour.

I suppose I shall tax your powers of belief if I tell you many more of Middy's doings. But truly he was a strange cat, and you may as well be patient, for you will not soon hear of his equal. The captain was much given to rifle practice, and used to love to go ashore and shoot at a mark. On one of his trips he allowed Middy to accompany him, for the simple reason, I suppose, that Middy decided to go and got on board the dinghy when the captain did. Once ashore, the marksman selected a fine large rock as a rest for his rifle, and opened fire upon his target. At the first shot or two Middy seemed a little surprised, but showed no disposition to run away. After the first few rounds, however, he seemed to have made up his mind that since the captain was making all the racket it must be entirely right and proper, and nothing about which a cat need bother his head in the least. So, as if to show how entirely he confided in the captain's judgment and good intentions, that imperturbable cat calmly lay down, curled up, and went to sleep in the shade of the rock over which the captain's rifle was blazing and cracking about once in two minutes. If anybody was ever acquainted with a cooler or more self-possessed cat I should be pleased to hear the particulars.

I wish that this chronicle could be confined to nothing but our shipmate's feats of daring and nerve. But, unfortunately, he was not always blameless in his conduct. When he got hungry he was apt to forget his position as midshipman, and to behave just like any cat with an empty stomach. Or perhaps he may have done just what any hungry midshipman does under the circumstances; I do not quite know what a midshipman does under all circumstances and so I cannot say. But here is one of this cat midshipman's exploits. One afternoon, on our way home, we were working along

with a head wind and sea toward Wood Island, a haven
for many of the small yachts between Portland and the
Shoals. The wind was light and we were a little late in
making port. But as we were all agreed that it would be
pleasanter to postpone our dinner till we were at anchor,
the cook was told to keep things warm and wait till we
were inside the port before he set the table. Now, his
main dish that day was to be a fine piece of baked fish;
and, unfortunately, it was nearly done when we gave
orders to hold back the dinner. So he had closed the
drafts of his little stove, left the door of the oven open,
and turned into his bunk for a quiet doze – a thing which
every good sailor does on all possible occasions; for a
seafaring life is very uncertain in the matter of sleep, and
one never quite knows when he will lose some, nor how
much he will lose. So it is well to lay in a good stock of it
whenever you can.

It seems that Middy was on watch, and when he saw Charlie fast asleep he undertook to secure a little early dinner for himself. He evidently reasoned with himself that it was very uncertain when we should have dinner and he'd better get his while he could. He quietly slipped down to the stove, walked coolly up to the oven, and began to help himself to baked haddock.

He must have missed his aim or made some mistake in his management of the business, and, by some lucky chance for the rest of us, waked the cook. For, the first we knew, Middy came flying up the cabin companionway, followed by a volley of shoes and spoons and pieces of coal, while we could hear Charlie, who was rather given to unseemly language when he was excited, using the strongest words in his dictionary about 'that thief of a cat!'

'What's the matter?' we all shouted at once.

'Matter enough, sir!' growled Charlie. 'That little cat's eaten up half the fish! It's a chance if you get any dinner tonight, sir.'

You may be very sure that Middy got a sound wigging for that trick, but I am afraid the captain forgot to deprive him of his rations as he threatened. He was much too kindhearted.

The very next evening Middy startled us again by a most remarkable display of coolness and courage. After a weary thrash to windward all day, under a provokingly light breeze, we found ourselves tinder the lee of the little promontory at Cape Neddick, where we cast anchor for the night. Our supply of water had run very low, and so, just after sunset, two of the party rowed ashore in the tender to replenish our water keg, and by special permission Middy went with them.

It took some time to find a well, and by the time the jugs were filled it had grown quite dark. In launching the boat for the return to the yacht, by some ill luck a breaker caught her and threw her back upon the beach. There she capsized and spilled out the boys, together with their precious cargo. In the confusion of the moment, and the hurry of setting matters to rights, Middy was entirely forgotten, and when the boat again was launched, nobody thought to look for the cat. This time everything went well, and in a few minutes the yacht was sighted through the dusk. Then somebody happened to think of Middy! He was nowhere to be seen. Neither man remembered anything about him after the capsize. There was consternation in the hearts of those unlucky wights. To lose Middy was almost like losing one of the crew.

But it was too late and too dark to go back and risk another landing on the beach. There was nothing to be done but to leave poor Middy to his fate, or at least to wait until morning before searching for him.

But just as the prow of the boat bumped against the fender on the yacht's quarter, out from under the stern sheets came a wet, bedraggled, shivering cat, who leaped on board the yacht and hurried below into the warm cabin. In that moist adventure in the surf, Middy had taken care of himself, rescued himself from a watery grave, got on board the boat as soon as she was ready, and sheltered himself in the warmest corner. All this he had done without the least outcry, and without asking any help whatever. His self-reliance and courage were extraordinary.

Well, the pleasant month of cruising drew to a close, and it became a question what should be done with Middy. We could not think of turning him adrift in the cold world, although we had no fears but that so bright and plucky a cat would make a living anywhere. But we wanted to watch over his fortunes, and perhaps take him on the next cruise with us when he should have become a more settled and dignified Thomas. Finally, it was decided that he should be boarded for the winter with an artist, Miss Susan H, a friend of one of our party. She wanted a studio cat, and would be particularly pleased to receive so accomplished and travelled a character as Middy. So when the yacht was moored to the little wharf at Annisquam, where she always ended her cruises, and we were packed and ready for our journey to Boston, Middy was tucked into a basket and taken to the train. He bore the confinement with the same good sense which had marked all his life with us, though I think his feelings were hurt at the lack of confidence we showed in him. And, in truth, we were a little ashamed of it ourselves and when once we were on the cars somebody suggested that he be released from his prison just to see how he would behave. We might have known he would do himself credit. For when he had looked over his surroundings, peeped above the back of the seat at the passengers, taken a good look at the conductor, and counted the rest of the party to see that none of us was missing, Middy snuggled down upon the seat, laid his head upon the captain's knee, and slept all the way to Boston.

That was the last time I ever saw Middy. He was taken to his new boarding place in Boylston Street, where he lived very pleasantly for a few months, and made many friends by his pleasing manners and unruffled temper. But I suppose he found it a little chill in Boston. He was not quite at home in his aesthetic surroundings. I have always believed he sighed for the freedom of a sailor's life. He loved to sit by the open window when the wind was east, and seemed to be dreaming of faraway scenes. One day he disappeared. No trace of him was ever found. A great many things may have happened to him. But I never could get rid of the feeling that he went down to the wharves and the ships and the sailors, trying to find his old friends, looking everywhere for the stanch little *Eyvor*; and, not finding her, I am convinced that he shipped on some East Indianman and is now a sailor cat on the high seas.

Feline Affection

An anonymous writer in the scientific journal *Nature* describes a remarkable example of a cat's affection for her master.

In 1887, I was absent from Madras two months, and left in my quarters three cats, one of which, an English tabby, was a very gentle, affectionate creature. During my absence the quarters were occupied by two young gentlemen who delighted in teasing and frightening the cats. About a week before my return, the English cat had had kittens, which she carefully concealed behind book-shelves in the library. On the morning of my return I saw the cat and patted her as usual, and then left the house for about an hour. On returning, I found that the kittens were located in the corner of my dressing-room, where previous broods had been deposited and nursed. On questioning the servant as to how they came there, he at once replied, 'Sir, the old cat, taking one by one in her mouth, brought them here.' In other words, the mother had carried them one by one in her mouth from the library to the dressing-room, where they lay quite exposed.

I do not think I have heard of a more remarkable instance of reasoning and affectionate confidence in an animal, and I need hardly say that the latter manifestation gave me great pleasure. The train of reasoning seems to have been as follows, 'Now that my master has returned, there is no risk of the kittens being injured by the two young savages in the house, so I will take them out for my protector to see and admire, and keep them in the corner in which all my former pets have been nursed in safety.'

Solomon and Sheba

DOREEN TOVEY

The day Sheba chased a gnat behind the picture over the bureau and left a row of black footprints up the wall Charles said it wasn't fair to blame the cats for everything. It wasn't her fault, he said, that when it flew past she happened to be looking up the chimney and had her paws covered in soot. I must remember that Siamese were not as other cats, and make allowance for their verve and curiosity.

He didn't say that when we put down the new stair-carpet and Solomon, busily showing Sheba how Strong he was, ripped the daylights out of the bottom-tread while we were still hammering down the top. He said Solomon was a damblasted little pest and if he wasn't careful he'd end up in the Cats' Home. Neither did it improve matters when I, to protect the rest of the carpet until Solomon got tired of sharpening his claws on it, made a set of stair-pads out of folded copies of *The Times*. The idea was to put a pad on each stair whenever we were going out. It worked for a few days – then one morning Charles, dashing up at the last moment to fetch his wallet, slipped on the top copy and slid from top to bottom on his neck. Both Solomon and I were in the dog-house then, and although it didn't worry me unduly – Charles, who is six feet tall, falls down the cottage stairs,

225

which are steep and narrow, quite regularly, and I would get the blame even if I were on the top of Everest at the time – Solomon was quite put out about it.

While Sheba comforted Charles in the hall, walking up and down on his stomach and asking anxiously if he were Dead, Solomon sat at the top of the stairs delivering a long Siamese monologue about the injustice of it all. Sheba Clawed Things, he said, and Nobody Complained About Her. She did too. The underside of the spare room arm chair sagged like a jelly bag where Sheba, when she first woke up in the morning, dragged herself round and round on her back by way of exercise – and all Charles said about that was that we had to make allowance for her high spirits.

She Knocked Things Down and Hit People Too, wailed Solomon. You could tell when he got to that bit by the pitch of his voice. Always powerful, it rose to an ear-shattering roar when he was in the right and knew it. Solomon didn't knock things down and hit people. He couldn't climb high enough to start with. But Sheba, shinning like a mountain goat up the bookshelves either side of the fireplace, was always bombarding unwary visitors with dislodged encyclopaedias or law books. Lately I had begun to wonder whether that, too, was quite the accident she claimed it to be. It had certainly been no accident the night I was just in time to stop her crowning Solomon with a Benares brass pitcher. When I caught her she was standing on the arm of a chair trying as hard as she could to hook it off the mantelpiece with her paw while he, stretched out full length to warm his stomach, lay innocently asleep on the rug below.

Now, craning his neck over the landing to make sure everybody heard him, Solomon continued his tale of woe. Charles was Clumsy, he wailed, staring reproachfully down at the spot where Sheba, relieved to find that Charles was good for a few more years yet, was making the most of the occasion by treading vigorously on his waistcoat and assuring him that *she* was a good girl. Charles would have Fallen Down the Stairs even without the newspapers, yelled Solomon. Charles Fell Over Everthing. Charles Fell Off the Ladder only last Saturday. Nobody, said Solomon, with the mournful wail-cum-sniffle which meant that at that moment he was feeling particularly hard done by, could blame him for that. Charles had done it All By Himself.

Charles had indeed. He had been painting the eaves of the cottage, perched on the sloping hall roof, on a ladder that had a cracked leg and was – despite Father Adams's warning that he knew several blokes who had killed themselves like that – suspended by faith and a piece of ancient rope from the chimney-stack. Charles's own version of what happened was that he was just reaching up to put on the last brushful of paint, thinking to himself (he was given to making up tense little dramas to amuse himself while he worked), 'And at that moment, just as he reached out for the final handhold, there was a sharp crack of breaking rope and he fell like a stone into the abyss below' – when the rope did break. Not with a sharp crack. It unravelled slowly and sadistically before his very eyes as he stood helplessly on the top rung. He didn't fall into any abyss either. He landed on the hall roof with a thump that shook the cottage to its poor old foundations. When I rushed out, convinced that I was a widow at last, he was sitting despondently on the roof in a pool of pale-blue paint while, standing side by side on top of the coal-house, craning their necks like a couple of spectators at a Lord Mayor's Show, Solomon and Sheba anxiously inquired what he wanted to do that for.

Charles said I might not believe it, but as he slid down the roof after the crash he had seen – actually *seen* – that pair gallop down the path and scramble up on to the coal-house as if it were a grandstand. I believed it all right. So often in trouble themselves, there was nothing they liked better than sitting smugly by, tails wrapped primly round their front paws and expressions of pained incredulity on their faces, when somebody else was in the soup. I remember once when a dog chased a neighbour's kitten up the electricity post outside our garden wall. Solomon was hardly in a position to talk, after the incident of the fire brigade, while Sheba had lately developed her mother's habit of demanding to be rescued by Charles from every tree she came across. It made no difference. While Charles and I tried to solve the problem of getting a ladder safely balanced against the rounded post they sat side by side at the foot, their necks stuck out like giraffes to emphasize What A Long Way Up She Was, their eyes round as bottle stops, yelling encouragingly up at her that she was Very Silly To Do A Thing Like That and They Didn't Suppose We'd Ever Get Her Down Again. The fact that no sooner had Charles rescued the kitten than he had to go up again to fetch Solomon, who had meanwhile climbed the ladder himself by way of an experiment and was now stuck half way up bellowing his own head off, was quite incidental. It still left Sheba at the bottom nattering away happily about what a long way up *he* was and she didn't suppose we'd ever get *him* down either.

It was inevitable, of course, that their rubber-necking would one day lead them into trouble. It happened at a time when we had new neighbours in the next cottage and Sol and Sheba, consumed with their usual curiosity, were going up every day to see how they were getting on. We warned the people not to encourage them. Disaster, we said, would unfailingly follow. Solomon would wreck their stair-carpet or raid their pantry and Sheba would either go up their chimney or fall down their lavatory. They wouldn't listen. They hadn't met any Siamese before and they were fascinated, they said, by the way our two marched one behind the other down the garden path, greeted them with an airy bellow and proceeded to inspect the place as if they owned it.

Which, so far as we could see, made it entirely the Westons' own fault when they tried to fill their water-butt during a drought by means of a hosepipe sneaking illicitly through the delphiniums and lupins to the kitchen tap and Solomon and Sheba promptly gave them away to the entire village by sitting on the outhouse roof, gazing wide-eyed down at the bubbles, and loudly inviting passers by to come and see what they'd found. Father Adams, who was one of the people who did – years ago his grandfather had lived in the Westons' cottage and that, according to country politics, really gave him more right to walk up the front path than the Westons themselves, who were newcomers from town – said old man Weston turned all the colours of a shammylon when he saw he'd been found out. He hadn't been there long enough to know that practically everybody else – certainly Father Adams – filled their water-butts in exactly the same way, and for days he went round hardly daring to look anybody in the face. Which, as Aunt Ethel said the day Solomon ate her guinea pot of beauty cream, just showed the folly of having anything to do with Siamese at all.

We never managed to get the better of them ourselves. Every time we thought we had them weighed off, up they came with something new. Mouse-catching, for instance. No sooner had we got used to the routine of Sheba catching them and Solomon slinging them round our heads for hours than Sheba, feeling that Solomon was getting too much limelight, decided that she'd better tell us when she caught a mouse in future, so there would be no mistaking it was hers. The first time Solomon heard her coming under the new system, moaning like a travelling air-raid siren, he said it was ghosts and hid under the bath and we had an awful job to coax him out; but it wasn't long before he, in turn, thought up an even better gimmick. He ate the mouse. Not quietly, in a corner, but noisily on the hearth-rug, leaving us the head and tail as souvenirs. The next thing was that Sheba ate a mouse too, but her stomach wasn't as strong as Solomon's and she went straight out and sicked it up on the stairs. And so, as Charles said, life went on.

There was a period, just after Sugieh died and the kittens were beginning to feel their feet as individuals, when if we had visitors we just couldn't move for them, sitting solidly in people's laps, licking their iced cakes when they weren't looking, investigating their handbags and chatting to them under the bathroom door. They liked people so much that when we shut them in the hall one night because one of Charles's friends had a dark suit on and wasn't very fond of cats anyway they climbed the curtains, got out through a transom window which we didn't know was open, and appeared suddenly with their small smudgy faces pressed to the window of the sitting-room, gazing wistfully in like orphans of the storm.

A great success that was. Everybody cooed over them and gave them ice-cream and Charles's friend went home with a suit that looked as if it were made of angora. The next time they were shut out on account of visitors Solomon, remembering the ice-cream, promptly jumped out of a window again. This time, however, as all the hall windows were shut, old Bat Brains went upstairs and jumped out of the bedroom window. One visitor fainted on the spot when she saw him coming down, but he landed in a hydrangea and was quite unharmed. The only thing was that now Solomon had discovered that he could open windows by putting his fat little bullet-head under the catches and pushing them up, in addition to spreading twelve copies of *The Times* on the stairs any time we shut them out, we now had to tie up all the window-catches with string as well.

Though the cats drove visitors nearly mad with their attention when they first arrived, however, if anybody

stayed after eleven o'clock things were very different.
Then, retiring to the most comfortable armchair (if
anybody was sitting in it they just squeezed down
behind him and kept turning round and round till he got
out; it never failed), they curled up and ostentatiously
tried to go to sleep. Tried was the operative word. Any
time anybody looked across at the chair there would be
at least one Siamese regarding them with half-raised
head, one eye open and a pained expression that clearly
indicated it was time they went home, Some People were
tired. If this had no effect, in due course Solomon would
sit up, yawn noisily and subside again with a loud sigh
on top of Sheba. Few visitors missed that hint. Solomon
yawned like fat men belch – long, loudly and with gusto.
What was most embarrassing, though, was the way –
after lying for hours as if they'd been working all day in
a chain gang – they suddenly perked up the moment
people did start to go. It wouldn't have been so bad if

they'd just politely seen them off at the door, the way Sugieh used to do. These two sat in the hall and bawled to people to hurry up – and as we shepherded people to the front gate they could be seen quite plainly through the window, hilariously chasing one another over the chairs by way of celebration.

To be quite honest, by that time the visitors usually weren't looking with such a kindly eye on the cats either. There was the friend, for instance, who brought an old pair of stockings for playing with the cats and left her best ones in our bedroom for safety. She expected the old ones to be ruined, and she was right. Solomon gave her a friendly nip in the ankle while we were having tea and bang they went. Unfortunately the bedroom door wasn't properly shut and while Sheba was, of her own accord, bringing the new ones down for the lady they went bang too, hitched up in a snag on the stairs.

There was the friend who unthinkingly left her car keys on the hall table. An innocent enough gesture – except that that was the time when Solomon was being an Alsatian dog and carrying things round in his mouth and it took us two hours to find where he had put them. Down the clock-golf hole on the lawn.

There was the cactus which disappeared mysteriously from its pot while its owner, who had just been given it by another friend, was calling on us for a cup of tea. Charles said if that didn't prove Solomon wasn't right in the head nothing did, but as a matter of fact it wasn't Solomon. It was Sheba, as we discovered later when we started raising cactus ourselves and had to lock them in the bathroom every night for safety while she howled under the door for just a little one to play marbles with.

It was Solomon, though, alone and unaided, who killed the fur coat. We laughed at the look of awe on his face the first time he saw it, and the way he immediately put up his back and offered to fight. We didn't give it a thought as the owner, patting him on the head and saying it was only a coat little man, tossed it nonchalantly on to the hall chair. But Solomon did. As soon as he'd had his share of the crab sandwiches he went out and killed it so dead I shudder even now to think how much it cost us to have it repaired.

We kept a strong guard on fur coats after that. Whenever one arrived Charles held Solomon in the kitchen while I personally locked it in the wardrobe and then locked the bedroom door. Even so I had qualms the night someone arrived wearing a particularly fine leopard coat and Solomon, as soon as supper was over, disappeared quietly into the hall. As soon as I could I slipped out too, to check. Everything seemed all right. The bedroom door was still firmly locked and when I spoke to him Solomon, sitting innocently on the hall table and gazing out into the night, said he was only looking for foxes.

It wasn't until the visitor, getting ready to go, started looking round the hall saying it was funny but she could have sworn she left it on the chest that I realized I hadn't taken her hat up to the bedroom as well – and by that time it was too late. It had – or rather it had had – a smart black cock's feather cockade on one side. When we picked it up, from under the same chair that had once concealed Aunt Ethel's famous telegram, all the feathers fell off.

By the time Solomon was six months old he had, despite his unpromising beginnings, grown into one of the most handsome Siamese we had ever seen. True he still had spotted whiskers and big feet and walked like Charlie Chaplin. But he had lost his puppy fat and was as lithe and sleek as a panther. His black, triangular mask – except for one solitary white hair right in the middle which he said he'd got through worrying over Sheba – shone like polished ebony. His eyes, set slantwise above high, Oriental cheekbones, were a brilliant sapphire and remarkable even for a Siamese. When he lay on the garden wall with his long black legs drooping elegantly over the edge he looked, according to Father Adams, exactly like a sheik in one of them Eastern palaces.

Father Adams, who was a great fan of Ethel M. Dell's, would have liked Solomon to be a sheik in the real romantic sense of the word. At that time he was still dreaming of making a fortune from cat-breeding and Solomon was so magnificent that there was nothing he would have liked more than to see him drag Mimi off into the hills by the scruff of her sleek cream neck and there found a race of Siamese that would, as he was always telling us, fetch ten quid apiece as easy as pie.

He was so disgusted when we had Solomon neutered that he wouldn't speak to us for a week – which was all very well; we didn't want to spoil Solomon's life either, but we had to share it with him and even our best friends wouldn't have lasted long in a house with an un-neutered Siamese. The only way we could have kept him – unless we let him wander, in which case a Siamese tom usually develops into a terrible fighter and rarely comes home at all – would have been outside in a stud-house.

When we asked Solomon about it he said he'd rather have beetles than girls. And cream cakes, he added, casting a speculative eye at the tea-trolley. And sleeping in our bed, he said that night, burrowing determinedly under the blankets to find my head.

That settled it. We could as soon imagine Solomon a stud tom as pretending to be a lion at the zoo. The following weekend he was neutered, and Sheba along with him, and not a scrap of trouble did we have with either of them except in the matter of Sheba's stitches. Two she had, and the vet who did the operation – a town one this time; not for one moment did we attach any blame to the vet who did Sugieh's operation, but it seemed fairer all round to have Sheba done by someone else – said we could easily take them out ourselves on the tenth day. Just snip here and there, he said, pull smartly – and the job was done.

It might have been with normal cats, but not with Sheba. She wasn't going to have any ham-fisted amateurs handling her, she said. Every time we approached her with the scissors she fled to the top shelf of the bookcase and barricaded herself in. Even Charles couldn't get her to come down. She liked him very much, she assured him from behind the Britannicas – but not her stitches, if he didn't mind. He could practise on Solomon, Mimi or even me. She wanted a real doctor. After the night when the stitches began to itch and she lay on our bed first trying to get them out herself and then letting Solomon have a go until the perpetual snick-snicking nearly drove us mad she got one, too. We could hardly ask the local vet to do the job, as he hadn't done the operation, so the next morning we rang Doctor Tucker, who came over and obliged at once. Sheba didn't run away from him. She told him at great length what we'd tried to do to her and did he think he ought to report it to the Medical Association. Then, while he snipped and pulled with the self-same scissors we had tried to use, she stood quietly on the table, her eyes happily crossed, and purred.

That, we thought, was the end of our troubles. The cats were growing up now. They had their little idiosyncrasies of course. Like Sheba's habit of turning out the vegetable rack every night, followed by complaints from our new help that it wasn't her job in other houses to fish sprouts and squashed tomatoes from under the cooker every morning. Not that it mattered much because she gave us notice quite soon anyway on account of Solomon's habit of walking over floors as soon as she'd scrubbed them.

Sheba was jolly pleased when she went. Now, she said – and how right she was – she'd be able to file sprouts under the stove until they smelled real high before anybody moved them. Solomon was pleased. She kept throwing the floor-cloth at him, he said, and if he hadn't been a gentleman – in the *highest* sense of the word, he said, ignoring Sheba's aside to Charles that he Wasn't Any More Was He, Not Since His Operation? – he'd have bitten her. Charles was pleased. If she hadn't gone, he said, judging by the looks she gave him when he asked her to empty the ashtrays, she'd have been throwing the floor cloth at him next. The only one who wasn't pleased was me – and I was too busy doing the housework to complain.

There was Solomon's keen interest in things mechanical which led him to follow the vacuum-cleaner like a bloodhound, with his nose glued firmly to the carpet, watching the bits disappear inside. Come to think of it, it was a good thing the help wasn't around the day he decided to experiment with that and, while I was moving a chair, poked his ball of silver paper curiously into the works. I turned round just in time to see a long black paw disappearing under the front and to hurl myself at the switch like a bomb.

Mrs Terry wouldn't have done that. She'd have screamed, thrown her apron over her head and fainted, the way she did when she removed the guard from the electric fire in the sitting-room for cleaning and Solomon, with happy memories of Mum, promptly walked over and stuck his rear against it. The only result of that incident had been that, for a while, Solomon's tail, indented in two places by the electric bars, had looked more like that of a poodle than a Siamese and Sheba had made him cross by pretending to be frightened every time she saw it. What might have happened with the vacuum I hardly dared to think.

These though, as I have said, were idiosyncrasies such as all Siamese owners experience. So long as we got up at five in the morning to let them out – otherwise Sheba knocked the lamp off the dressing-table and Solomon bit us; so long as we only ate chocolates wrapped in silver paper and let Solomon have every single piece – he sulked like mad when somebody gave us a 4lb box for Christmas without an inch of silver paper among them: Done It On Purpose he said they had, watching disconsolately every time the box was opened, and couldn't we eat them faster than that; so long as we kept a box of All Bran permanently on the kitchen floor to fill the corners when he felt peckish – if we didn't he was liable to get in the cupboard and look for it himself with disastrous results; so long as we remembered little things like that we had no trouble at all. Real little home birds they were. Always running in to see that we hadn't gone for a walk without them – or even more important, that we weren't eating something behind their backs.

Which made it all the more worrying the morning I called the cats and instead of the usual mad stampede to see what was for breakfast only Sheba appeared, looking very small and forlorn and nattering anxiously that Solomon had vanished; she'd looked all over the place for him and she didnt know where he could be.

We didn't know it then but Solomon, tired of the chains of civilization, had gone to be an explorer – and, as explorers sometimes do, he had met with a hazard. When I found him an hour later, after scouring the countryside till I was practically on my knees, he was in a field more than a mile away with a pair of large and angry geese. When I panted up he was crouching in a corner bawling his head off about what he'd do if they came any nearer, but he didn't fool them – or me. He was scared stiff. His ears stuck up like a pair of horrified exclamation marks. His eyes were nearly popping out of his head. When I called him he gave a long, despairing wail which clearly signified that if I didn't hurry up the cannibals would get him, and he wasn't half in a fix.

I got him out of that by wading knee-deep in a bed of stinging-nettles, leaning over a barbed-wire fence and hauling him out by the scruff of his neck. From the look on the faces of those geese it was obvious there wasn't time to go round by the gate. He never learned, of course. No sooner was he safely on my shoulder and the geese out of earshot than the old bounce was back. All the way home I had a monologue right in my ear about what they said to him and what he said back – punctuated halfway by a decision, which I nipped in the bud by grabbing his tail and hanging on to it firmly, to go right back and tell them some more.

By the time we got home Solomon, in his own mind at least, was a budding Marco Polo. And from then on we had hardly a moment's peace. Summoned by a wail that turned my blood cold when I heard it, I rescued him from one emergency after another. Once, under the impression that she was running away from him, he chased a cow that was being tormented by flies. That was fine fun while it lasted, tearing across the field with the wind in his tail and his long black legs going like a racehorse – until the cow turned round, saw Buffalo Bill capering cockily at her heels, and chased him instead.

I rescued him that time from a handy wall, doing a fine imitation of the Stag at Bay with the cow's horns about an inch from his trembling black nose. The time he frightened a little lamb, though, he wasn't so lucky. His nearest point of escape then was through a hedge which topped a steep bank above the woods, and by the time he made it the lamb's mother was so close behind he couldn't stop to look for a proper way through. As I toiled wearily up through the woods in answer to his yell for help he appeared dramatically on the skyline, leapt into space, and landed ignominiously in a pool of mud.

That taught him nothing either. The very next day I saw him – in his own inimitable way, which meant laboriously hiding behind every blade of grass he came across and crawling across the open bits on his stomach – tracking a small kitten into the self-same woods. I let him go that time. His dusky face was alight with eagerness, there was such an Excelsior light in his eyes – and he couldn't, I thought, get into trouble with a little kitten like that.

That was where I was wrong. A few minutes later there was a volcanic explosion, a mad crashing of branches, silence – and then, once more, the familiar sound of Solomon yelling for help. Creeping stealthily through the woods he had, it seemed, come across his enemy from the farmyard, doing a bit of mousing. Judging by the way the tom went streaking up the road as I dashed into the woods he was just as alarmed as Solomon by the encounter – and indeed it wasn't that that Columbus was belly-aching about. It was that, just as he had taken refuge up a tree, so had the kitten. Up the same tree, Solomon had made it first and was clinging for dear life six feet up while the kitten, unable to pass him, was directly under his tail. Solomon, in all his glory, a magnificent, intimidating specimen of a male Siamese, was howling because a tiny kitten, no bigger than a flea, wouldn't let him get down.

After that Solomon kept away from the woods for a while. He took to sitting on the garden wall instead, pretending, when we asked him why he hadn't gone exploring, that he was Waiting for a Friend. That, unfortunately, was how he came to get interested in horses. Unfortunately – because when Solomon got interested in anything he invariably wanted a closer look. Unfortunately – because it wasn't long before the owner of the local riding-school was ringing us up to ask whether we would mind keeping him in while her pupils went by. He was frightening the horses, she said. Little Patricia had already fallen into our stinging-nettles twice, and her mother didn't like it.

When we said, somewhat indignantly, that cats didn't frighten horses, she said ours did. She said he lurked in the grass until the first one had gone by, then dashed out into the road and pranced along behind him. It looked, she said, almost as if he was imitating the horse – though that of course was ridiculous. The first horse was all right because he couldn't see the cat; the ones behind, she said – and we could quite see her point – nearly had hysterics.

We saw to it that, after that, Solomon did his imitations from the hall window when the riding-school went by. Unfortunately, while it was easy enough to tell when they were coming – what with the trampling of hoofs and instructions to people to watch their knees or keep their eyes on their elbows they made, according to Father Adams, more noise than the ruddy Campbells – solitary riders were different. Sometimes we were in time to stop Trigger the Second following his latest idol down the lane. More often the first we knew that a horse had passed that way was when once again Solomon was missing.

It was very worrying. Sometimes it would be a couple of hours or more before he came plodding back on his long thin legs, looking rather sheepish and trying to slip through the gate so that he could pretend he'd been there all the time. We tried everything we could think of, short of a cage, to curb this latest craze. We even bought some goldfish, seeing it was things that moved he liked, and set up a special tank for him in the sitting-room.

Sheba and Charles thought they were wonderful. They sat in front of the tank for ages goggling like a couple of tennis fans as the fish flipped and glided lazily through the water. Solomon, however, when he found there was no way in at the top or sides and that they didn't run away when he looked at them, lost interest and slipped silently out. Charles was too intent on the fish to see him go, or to notice the lone, red-coated rider clopping up the lane; and I was in the kitchen. The first I knew of his latest escapade was when the phone rang and a farmer from the other end of the valley said he didn't know whether I knew it but that black-faced cat of ours had just gone by following one of the huntsmen. He was going it well, he said, stepping it out, like a proper little Arab. But the horse was a kicker with a red ribbon on its tail and he didn't....

I didn't wait to hear any more. I dropped the phone and ran. When I caught up with them Solomon was still, unknown to the rider, following doggedly along behind that pair of wicked-looking hoofs. The huntsman stared in admiration as I picked him up. Plucky little devil, he said, to have followed all that way. Ought to have been a horse himself. He didn't know me, of course, or Solomon, from Adam. He looked a little alarmed when, holding old Bat Ears firmly by the scruff of his neck, I said it was a remark like that which started all this horse business in the first place.

Cats of Honour

GENERAL SIR THOMAS
EDWARD GORDON

Gordon, a British officer stationed in India, wrote this
piece in 1906.

For twenty-five years, an oral addition to the written
standing orders of the native guard at Government
House near Poona had been communicated
regularly from one guard to another on relief, to the
effect that any cat passing out of the front door after dark
was to be regarded as His Excellency, the Governor, and
to be saluted accordingly. The meaning of this was that
Sir Robert Grant, Governor of Bombay, had died there in
1838 and on the evening of the day of his death a cat was
seen to leave the house by the front door and walk up
and down a particular path, as it had been the
Governor's habit to do after sunset.

A Hindu sentry had observed this, and he mentioned it
to others of his faith, who made it a subject of
superstitious conjecture, the result being that one of the
priestly class explained the mystery of the dogma of the
transmigration of the soul from one body to another, and
interpreted the circumstance to mean that the spirit of
the deceased Governor had entered into one of the house
pets. It was difficult to fix on a particular one, and it was
therefore decided that every cat passing out of the main

242

entrance after dark was to be treated with due respect and the proper honours. The decision was accepted without question by all the native attendants and others belonging to Government House. The whole guard, from sepoy to sibadar, fully acquiesced to it, and an oral addition was made to the standing orders that the sentry at the front door 'present arms to any cat passing out there after dark'.

Dr Johnson's Cat

Dr Samuel Johnson (1709-1784) lived for eleven years at Number 17, Gough Square, London, a home he shared with his beloved cat, Hodge. It was in this house that Johnson produced the dictionary for which he is famous. Hodge kept him company as he laboured for many years on this mammoth task. In his dictionary, Johnson defines the Cat in these words:

'A domestick animal that catches mice, commonly reckoned by naturalists the lowest order of the leonine species.'

Naturalists may have considered the cat a lowly animal, but there is no doubt that the great lexicographer held Hodge in very high regard. Johnson's affection for cats in general, and Hodge in particular, was documented by his biographer, James Boswell, in his book *The Life of Samuel Johnson*, which was published in 1799. As a non-cat person himself (and reputedly allergic to felines), Boswell was intrigued by his friend's fondness for Hodge.

He wrote:

'I never shall forget the indulgence with which he treated Hodge, his cat; for whom he himself used to go out and buy òysters, lest the servants, having that trouble, should take a dislike to the poor creature. I am, unluckily, one of those who have an antipathy to a cat, so that I am uneasy when in the room with one; and I own, I frequently suffered a good deal from the presence of this same Hodge. I recollect him one day scrambling up Dr Johnson's breast, apparently with much satisfaction, while my friend, smiling and half-whistling, rubbed down his back, and pulled him by the tail; and when I observed he was a fine cat, saying, "Why, yes, Sir, but I have had cats whom I liked better than this"; and then, as if perceiving Hodge to be out of countenance, adding, "but he is a very fine cat, a very fine cat indeed."'

We do not know exactly when Hodge passed away, but we are told that, when his cat was dying, Dr Johnson went out to find some valerian (a plant similar to catnip) to make Hodge's last hours as pleasant as possible.

A memorial to Hodge, in the form of a bronze life-size statue by sculptor Jon Buckley, was unveiled on 26 September 1997 by the Lord Mayor of London, Sir Roger Cook. The metal Hodge, sitting on a dictionary with oysters at his feet, keeps splendid guard opposite the house he and his devoted master called home for so many years.

Acknowledgments

All possible care has been taken to make full acknowledgment in every case where material is still in copyright. If errors have occurred, they will be corrected in subsequent editions if notification is sent to the publisher. Grateful acknowledgment is made for permission to reprint the following:

MRS BOND'S CATS from *All Things Bright and Beautiful* by James Herriot. Reproduced by permission of David Higham Associates Limited. Copyright © 1973, 1974 by James Herriot.

INCIDENT ON EAST NINTH by Jill Drower. Reproduced by permission of the author.

Extract from THE CHERRY TREE by Derek Tangye (Michael Joseph, 1986) copyright © Derek Tangye, 1986.

ALAS, POOR TIDDLES, WE KNEW HIM WELL… by Andrew Parsons © 2000. Reproduced by permission of News International Syndication.

MY BOSS THE CAT by Paul Gallico. Copyright © Mathemata Ag. 1964. Reproduced by permission of Gillon Aitken Associates Limited.

THE FAT CAT by Q. Patrick. Copyright © 1944 by Q. Patrick. Reproduced by permission of Curtis Brown Limited.